Study Guide to Accompany

Baking and Pastry
Mastering the Art and Craft

Second Edition

The Culinary Institute of America

WILEY
JOHN WILEY & SONS, INC.

This book is printed on acid-free paper. ∞

Published by John Wiley & Sons, Inc., Hoboken, New Jersey
Published simultaneously in Canada

For general information on our other products and services or for technical support, please contact our Customer Care Department within the United States at (800) 762-2974, outside the United States at (317) 572-3993 or fax (317) 572-4002.

Wiley also publishes its books in a variety of electronic formats. Some content that appears in print may not be available in electronic books. For more information about Wiley products, visit our web site at www.wiley.com.

This material may be reproduced for testing or instructional purposes by instructors using the text *Baking and Pastry, Second Edition*, by The Culinary Institute of America
(ISBN: 978-0-470-05591-5)

Library of Congress Cataloging-in-Publication Data:

ISBN: 978-0-470-25868-2

Printed in the United States of America

10 9 8 7 6 5 4 3 2

Contents

CHAPTER 1

CAREER OPPORTUNITIES FOR BAKING AND PASTRY PROFESSIONALS

Chapter Overview

Baking originated thousands of years ago and it is integral to human history and still is the source of the most basic foodstuffs. Bread's importance can be seen in the way governments regulated its production, quality, weight, and price. Bakers established the first trade guilds in Rome in 150 b.c.e.

Chapter Objectives

After reading and studying this chapter, you should be able to:

➤ Define in brief how the role of the pastry chef evolved within Classical Cuisine.
➤ Describe the breadth of career opportunities available for baking and pastry professionals.
➤ Discuss the impact a formal education in baking and pastry can have on career paths in these disciplines.
➤ Discuss the importance of continuing education to baking and pastry professionals.
➤ Define various kinds of certification available to baking and pastry professionals.
➤ Talk about the benefits of networking and how they can impact a baking and pastry career.
➤ Outline the basic aspects of a baking and pastry business and how mastering them can impact success.

Study Outline

Key Terms and Concepts
Career Opportunities & Continuing Education

wholesale bakeshops	commercial bakeries	pastry chef
restaurant pastry chef	formal education	continuing education
physical assets	networking	human resources
commitment to service		

Certification

Retailers Bakery Association (RBA)	American Culinary Federation (ACF)
Certified Journey Baker (CJB)	Certified Baker (CB)
Certified Decorator (CD)	Certified Bread Baker (CBB)
Working Pastry Chef (WPC)	Certified Executive Pastry Chef (CECF)
Certified Master Baker (CMB)	Certified Master Pastry Chef (CMPC)

Self Study Questions

True/False

_____ 1. Bakers were among the first tradesmen organized into guilds.

_____ 2. In larger operations, like wholesale bakeshops, pastries and cakes are often sold to supermarkets.

_____ 3. Many food producers maintain test kitchens to test products and formulas and fine-tune them.

_____ 4. CJB stands for Certified Journey Baker, which is an entry level certification.

_____ 5. The exams administered by the RBA for certification, have only a practical (hands-on) component.

_____ 6. Both the RBA and the ACF have specific minimum criteria that must be met before you can apply for certification.

_____ 7. The first step to bringing expenses associated with physical assets under control is to run a business for one year and compare it to a business of the same size.

_____ 8. Current tastes have an effect on what people eat and where and how they want to eat.

Multiple Choice

1. Within the *brigade system* the production of pastries was the responsibility of the
    _____.
    - a. confiseur
    - b. boulanger
    - c. pâtissier
    - d. saucier

2. CMB as it pertains to training in the baking and pastry profession stands for:
    - a. Chef Mentor
    - b. Community Mentor of Baking
    - c. Certified Master Baker
    - d. Culinary Mastery of Baking

3. _____ is the highest certification granted by the ACF and involves a 10-day exam that combines a written and practical examination that covers classical and contemporary applications.
   a. Certified Master Baker (CMB)
   b. Certified Journey Baker (CJB)
   c. Certified Master Pastry Chef (CMPC)
   d. Certified Executive Pastry Chef (CEPC)

4. To properly manage time in the workplace one must:
   a. create an orderly work environment
   b. have meetings every day
   c. know how to send an email
   d. be able to use a piping bag

5. In an increasingly tight labor market, a generous _____ can make the difference in the caliber of employees any company or shop is able to attract and retail.
   a. work schedule
   b. benefits package
   c. holiday get-together
   d. break schedule

Fill in the Blank

1. Large businesses specializing in baking and pastry production can offer employees _____ and _____ that may not otherwise be available in a smaller operation.

2. The following are choices for certification established by the RBA: _____, _____, _____, _____.

3. The _____, and _____ have established standards for certifying bakers and pastry chefs.

4. All professionals must learn the foundations of the profession— _____ and _____, and _____.

5. Employees have a right to work in an environment that is free from _____, and with properly _____.

Written/Short Answer

1. Bakers will most often follow one of two paths, working in either:

2. Wholesale bakeshops sell finished or par-baked items, as well as unbaked and unformed doughs and batters, to a variety of outlets such as:

3. Grocery stores and department stores hire a significant number of baking and pastry professionals. Responsibilities may include:

4. Some of the responsibilities for which baking and pastry professionals are hired in research-and-development kitchens are:

5. Name four things a baking and pastry professional can do to hone skills in specialized areas while keeping up with new methods, ingredients techniques, products and business skills:

6. The skills required for managing time efficiently include:

7. Name six places to look for professional level courses and continuing education workshops:

Essay

1. In terms of time management in a business operation, what are considered to be the top five "time wasters" and what strategies can be used to combat them?

CHAPTER 2

INGREDIENT IDENTIFICATION

Chapter Overview

Choosing ingredients with care, based upon quality, seasonality, and other considerations, including cost, is a prerequisite for high-quality baked goods. Each ingredient has its own set of characteristics, and it is the pastry chef or baker's job to know how to handle all ingredients properly from the time they are received throughout each phase of storage, handling and preparation.

Chapter Objectives

After reading and studying this chapter, you should be able to:
- Explain the key differences between flours, grains and meals.
- Define the different types of flour commonly used in bakeshops.
- Define the different types of sugars, syrups, and other sweeteners commonly used in bakeshops.
- Define the different types of thickeners commonly used in bakeshops.
- Define a variety of dairy products and how their properties are applied in bakeshops.
- Identify the different size categories of eggs and the various forms in which they are used in bakeshops.
- Explain the properties of different oils, shortenings and other fats used in bakeshops.
- Describe the process of making chocolate and identify the different types of chocolate.
- Identify common leaveners and the different kinds of salts used in bakeshops.
- Identify the most common herbs and spices used in bakeshops.
- Identify a variety of nuts and seeds commonly used in bakeshops.
- Explain proper handling and storage of fresh produce.
- Identify a variety of apples, berries, citrus fruits, melons, pears, stone fruits, and exotic or tropical fruits used in bakeshops.
- Describe briefly how extracts, wines, cordials and liqueurs, coffee and tea are used in bakeshops.

Study Outline

Key Terms and Concepts
Flours, Grains and Meals

whole grains	milled grains	bran	germ
endosperm	milling	extraction rate	ash content
aging & bleaching	green flour	benzoyl peroxide	chlorine dioxide

bleached flour	oxidizing	enrichment	all-purpose flour
bread flour	high-gluten flour	clear flour	whole-wheat flour
durum flour	semolina	cake flour	pastry flour
cracked wheat vital	wheat gluten	medium rye flour	dark rye flour
pumpernickel flour	oat groats	oat flour	steel-cut oats
rolled oats	instant oats	buckwheat	kasha
spelt	millet	cornmeal	cornstarch
white rice	brown rice		

Sugars, Syrups, and other Sweeteners

pearl/decorating sugar	granulated sugar	superfine sugar
sanding sugar	brown sugar	turbinado sugar
confectioners' sugar	isomalt	corn syrup
dark corn syrup	glucose syrup	molasses
honey	malt syrup	diastatic malt syrup
non-diastatic malt syrup	golden syrup	maple syrup
inverted syrup		

Thickeners

thickener	gelatin	pectin	agar-agar
cornstarch	potato starch	arrowroot	tapioca
processed/refined starches			
modified/converted starches			

Dairy Products

homogenization	pasteurization	whole milk	reduced-fat milk
low-fat milk	fat-free milk	heavy/whipping cream	
light cream	evaporated milk	sweetened condensed milk	
nonfat dry milk	buttermilk	sour cream	
yogurt	crème fraiche	farmers and baker's cheeses	
ricotta cheese	ricotta impastata	cream cheese	
reduced-fat cream cheese		mozzarella cheese	
hard cheese		cheddar cheese	
Parmesan cheese		sweet butter	

Eggs

| dried eggs | pasteurized eggs | egg substitutes |

Oils, Shortenings, and Other Fats

vegetable oils	olive oils
nut oils	oil sprays
hydrogenated shortenings	emulsifying shortening/high-ratio shortening
margarine	lard

Chocolate

| chocolate liquor | cocoa butter |

cocoa powder
bittersweet chocolate
couverture chocolate
sweet chocolate
confectionery coating

unsweetened chocolate
semi-sweet chocolate
milk chocolate
white chocolate

Leaveners

active dry yeast
instant dry yeast
baking powder

rapid dry yeast
compressed fresh yeast
baking soda

Salt

| table salt | kosher salt | sea salt | rock salt/bay salt |

Herbs, Spices, and Flavorings

basil	chive	dill	oregano
marjoram	parsley	rosemary	allspice
caraway seed	anise seed	cardamom	cinnamon
cloves	nutmeg	peppercorns	black peppercorns white
peppercorns	mignonette	shot pepper	green peppercorns
pink peppercorns	vanilla beans	garlic	ginger

Nuts

almond	sweet almonds	bitter almonds	Brazil nut
cashew	chestnut	coconut	hazelnut
Macadamia nut	peanuts	pecan	pistachio nut
walnut	white walnut/butternut		black walnut

Seeds

| anise seeds | caraway seeds | poppy seeds | pumpkin seeds |
| sesame seeds | tahini | sunflower seeds | |

Fresh Produce

hydroponic growing	strawberries	raspberries	dewberries
mulberries	boysenberries	blackberries	blueberries
currants	elderberries	gooseberries	grapes
cranberries	juice oranges	eating oranges	bitter oranges
mandarin oranges	grapefruits	lemons	Persian limes
kumquats	cantaloupes	muskmelons	watermelons
winter melons	honeydew melons	Persian melons	Asian pears
Bartlett pears	Bosc pears	D'Anjou pears	Seckel pears
peaches	nectarines	apricots	plums
Greengage plums	Damson plums	prune plums	bananas
guavas	kiwis	lychees	mangoes
papayas	passion fruits	persimmon	rhubarb

Fuyu persimmon   pomegranates   star fruits   cherries
Hachiya persimmon   Bing cherries   Royal Ann cherries
Queen Anne cherries

Self Study Questions

True/False

_____ 1. Wheat flour is the most common type of flour used in bakeshops.

_____ 2. Enrichment is the process that separates the wheat kernel into its three parts, bran, germ and endosperm.

_____ 3. Bakers refer to freshly milled four as "green flour."

_____ 4. Oat flour contains a high percentage of gluten.

_____ 5. Enriched flour dramatically affects baking performance.

_____ 6. Rye flour behaves quite differently from wheat flour in baking because the manners in which the two grains are milled are quite different from one another.

_____ 7. Dark corn syrup contains refiner's syrup.

_____ 8. Light cream contains 35% milk fat.

_____ 9. Confectionery chocolate is 15 percent chocolate liquor, 15 percent cocoa butter, and 70 percent sugar.

_____ 10. Gelatin is processed from the skin and bones and connective tissue of animals.

Multiple Choice

1. _____ is the percent of flour obtained after a grain has been milled.
   a. Vital wheat gluten
   b. Ash content
   c. Extraction rate
   d. Endosperm

2. _____ is a milling standard that determines the mineral (inorganic) material remaining in the flour after milling.
   a. Ash content
   b. Aging and bleaching
   c. Oxidizing
   d. Enrichment

3. _____ are produced from liquid fats that have been chemically altered under pressure using purified hydrogen to make them solid at room temperature.
    a. Nut oils
    b. Olive oils
    c. Oil sprays
    d. Hydrogenated shortenings

4. Ripe fruits and vegetables should be refrigerated. Unless otherwise specified, produce should be kept at a temperature of _____ with relative humidity of

    _____.
    a. 30° to 35°F/-1° to 2°C and 80 to 90 percent
    b. 32° to 35°F/0° to 2°C and 75 to 80 percent
    c. 40° to 45°F/4° to 7°C and 80 to 90 percent
    d. 40° to 45°F/4° to 7°C and 75 to 80 percent

5. _____ is a plant in the ginger family. Each of its pods contains 15 to 20 small seeds.
    a. allspice
    b. cloves
    c. nutmeg
    d. cardamom
    e. peppercorns

Fill in the Blank

1. Milled grains are polished to remove the _____, _____, and/or _____. They may have a longer shelf life than whole grains, but some of their nutritive value is lost during processing.

2. Enriched flour has nutrients replaced that were lost during milling. Nutrients added include _____, _____, _____, _____ and _____.

3. The three types of rye flour are: _____, _____, and

    _____ _____.

4. Corn syrup contains _____ dextrose.

5. Four cultured milk products produced by inoculating milk or cream with a bacterial strain under precisely controlled conditions are: _____, _____, _____ _____, and _____.

Matching

1. Matching – *Flours, grains and meals*

All-purpose flour _____

Whole wheat flour _____

Clear flour _____

Cake flour _____

Semolina _____

High-gluten flour _____

a. _____ is a hard wheat flour made from the endosperm has a darker color than bread or high-gluten flour and is typically used in rye breads. The protein content of clear flour ranges from 13 to 15 percent.

b. _____ is milled from the entire endosperm; it is used for bagels and hard rolls. Its protein content is typically 13 to 14 percent.

c. _____ is a more coarsely ground durum wheat flour, used most typically in pasta making.

d. _____ is blend of hard and soft wheat flours milled from the endosperm of the wheat kernel; the specific blend varies from region to region. Southern all-purpose flour generally has more soft wheat than all-purpose flours in other parts of the county. The protein content in all-purpose flour can range from 8 to 12 percent.

e. _____ is a hard wheat flour milled from the entire wheat kernel, including the bran and germ; because the germ is high in lipids, whole-wheat flour can quickly become rancid. Its protein content ranges from 14 to 16 percent.

f. _____ is a soft wheat flour with a protein content ranging from 6 to 9 percent. It is used for cakes and cookies

1. Matching - *Sugars, syrups, and other sweeteners*

Isomalt _____

Superfine sugar _____

Confectioners' sugar _____

Granulated sugar _____

Turbinado sugar _____

Brown sugar _____

a. _____ has very small crystals and dissolves quickly. It is sometimes used in cake batters and in meringues.

b. _____ is a coarse granular partially refined sugar with a light brown color and a very mild molasses taste.

c. _____ is a white crystalline "sugar-free" sweetener made from sucrose, used in diabetic baking. Because it does not break down when heated and absorbs very little water; some pastry chefs like to use it for pulled sugar work.

d. _____, also called powdered, or icing sugar, is granulated sugar ground to a powder, with cornstarch added (up to 3 percent by weight) to keep it from caking.

e. _____ is granulated sugar with added molasses.

f. _____ is pure refined sucrose derived from either sugarcane, or from sugar beets. Granulated sugar has small, evenly sized crystals, and it is the most commonly used sugar in the bakeshop.

Written/Short Answer

1. Name the various methods used for milling:

2. Name five other grains from which flours are made that add distinctive flavors and textures to baked goods:

3. Name the two products used to chemically age and bleach flour.

4. Dark corn syrup contains:

5. Name the six sizes by which eggs are classified:

6. Name six different ingredients added to baked products that are added to provide leavening:

7. List the seven most commonly available apple varieties.

Essay

1. How is wheat classified?

2. Define the term "thickener."

3. Define homogenization and pasteurization as they pertain to milk.

CHAPTER 3

EQUIPMENT IDENTIFICATION

Chapter Overview
Just as an artist learns to master all the instruments necessary for painting, sculpting, or drawing, bakers and pastry chefs learn to master a variety of small tools and large equipment. These devices are as important as you own fingers – quite literally an extension of your hands. Tools and equipment of all sorts represent one of the biggest investments in the professional bakeshop or kitchen.

Chapter Objectives
After reading and studying this chapter, you should be able to:
> - Identify the various kinds of scaling and measuring tools used in professional bakeshops.
> - Identify the various kinds of cutting tools used in professional bakeshops.
> - Identify the variety of other small tools used in professional bakeshops.
> - Identify the various kinds of hand tools for sifting, straining, and pureeing used in professional bakeshops.
> - Identify the various kinds of tools for break baking used in professional bakeshops.
> - Identify the various kinds of tools for pastries and cookies used in professional bakeshops.
> - Identify the various kinds of tools for décor work used in professional bakeshops.
> - Identify the various kinds of tools used for confectionery and décor work in professional bakeshops.
> - Identify the various kinds of bakeware used in professional bakeshops.
> - Identify the various kinds of kitchen equipment and refrigeration used in professional bakeshops.

Study Outline

Key Terms and Concepts
Scaling and Measuring Tools

Tare	beam balance	fulcrum
spring scale	digital scale	graduated pitcher
measuring cups	measuring spoons	dry measuring cups
stem-type thermometer	probe thermometer	instant-read
thermometerdigital thermometer		

candy/sugar/deep fat thermometer

Cutting Tools

chef's/French knife	utility knife	paring knife
slicer	mandoline	

Other Small Tools

grater	citrus zester	rasp
swivel-bladed peeler	lemon reamer	apple corer
slotted/perforated spoon	spider/skimmer	paddle
tongs	balloon whip	flat whip
rubber spatula	plastic bowl scraper	metal spatula
scoop	melon baller	ladle

Hand Tools for Sifting, Straining and Puréeing

sieve	strainer	food mill
drum sieve/tamis	conical sieve	colander
cheesecloth		

Tools for Bread Baking

lame	bench knife	couche
loaf pan	banneton	peel

Tools for Pastries and Cookies

rolling pin	rod-and-bearing rolling pin	straight/French rolling pin
tapered rolling pin	marzipan rolling pin	basket-weave rolling pin
cookie cutter	dough docker	pastry wheel
Springerle rolling pin		

Tools for Décor Work

pastry bag	piping tip	parchment paper cone
cake comb	rubber decorating comb	wire cooling rack
turntable		

Tools for Confectionery and Décor Work

heavy copper pot	fondant funnel	chocolate molds
dipping tools	chocolate cutter	caramel bars
guitar	transfer sheets	marzipan modeling tool
gum paste modeling tool	airbrush	acetate sheets
sugar lamp	blow dryer	blown sugar pump

Bakeware

hotel pan	sheet pan	cake pan

Kitchen Equipment and Refrigeration

blender	immersion blender	vertical chopping machine
food chopper	buffalo chopper	food processor
planetary mixer	spiral mixer	oblique mixer
conventional ovens	deck oven	steam-injection oven
convection oven	combi oven	microwave oven
proofer	retarder	walk-in
reach-in refrigerator	on-site refrigeration unit	portable refrigeration
electric ice cream machine	hand-cranked ice cream machine	
batch ice cream freezer	commercial ice cream maker	
vertical machines	horizontal machines	

Self Study Questions

True/False

_____ 1. To tare a spring scale, place the container for measuring the ingredients on the scale and turn the dial so that the pointer or arrow is aligned with zero.

_____ 2. Spring scales are designed to measure only large increments.

_____ 3. Severely dulled or damaged tools should be professionally re-ground to restore the edge.

_____ 4. Sanitizing the entire knife, including the handle, bolster, and blade is one way to help prevent cross-contamination of foods.

_____ 5. Hand held wire whips may have as few as ten wires or as many as twenty.

_____ 6. Scoops and ladles are used as portioning tools.

_____ 7. The numbers assigned to pastry tips do have a relationship to the diameter of the tip's opening: the bigger the number, the larger the opening.

_____ 8. Hotel pans are deeper than sheet pans, making them well-suited for use with hot water baths, in making custards and other preparations.

_____ 9. The speed settings for blenders may be as many as eighteen or as few as two, and are generally located in the base.

_____ 10. Deck ovens are only powered by gas or electricity.

Multiple Choice

1. _____ have a stainless steel platform set on an electronic base with digital display.
   a. Beam balances
   b. Spring scales
   c. Digital scales
   d. Baker's scales

2. _____ consist of plastic digital-read base with a metal probe on the end of a cord; some have an alarm setting to indicate that a specific temperature has been reached.
   a. Mercury thermometers
   b. Probe thermometers
   c. Stem-type thermometers
   d. Instant read thermometers

3. A/an _____ may be a hand tool or mechanical device. As a mechanical device it has an arm with three prongs that are inserted into the item, fixing it on a crank handle that drills it into a cylindrical blade that extracts the center.
   a. apple corer
   b. lemon reamer
   c. swivel-bladed peeler
   d. citrus zester

4. A _____ is a thin-arched razor blade clamped in a small stainless steel, wooden or plastic handle. It is used to score proofed yeast breads and rolls before baking to create patterns and designs on the crust.
   a. lame
   b. bench knife
   c. conical sieve
   d. slicer

5. _____ are large, flat wooden paddles designed for transferring doughs onto the deck of an oven.
   a. Metal spatulas
   b. Couches
   c. Bannetons
   d. Peels

Fill in the Blank

1. Candy thermometers should register from _____ and should be able to withstand temperatures up to _____.

2. The bowl of a ladle holds a specific volume, ranging from _____ to
_____ .

3. _____ and _____ are used to sift and aerate dry ingredients, as well as remove any large impurities from them.

4. A/an _____ is used to spray food colors onto confections and cakes.

5. A _____ is a rubber squeeze ball that fits in the palm of your hand attached to an aluminum tip. It is squeezed to blow air into sugar to create a "balloon" that may be shaped and molded by hand as it is expanded.

Matching

1. Matching – Hand tools for sifting, straining, and puréeing

Sieves and strainers _____
Food mill _____
Drum sieve _____
Conical sieve _____
Colander _____
Cheesecloth _____

a. _____ are stainless steel, aluminum, or plastic bowls pierced with holes used for straining or draining foods.

b. _____ consist of tinned-steel, nylon, or stainless-steel screen stretched over an aluminum or wood frame.

c. _____ and _____ are used to sift and aerate dry ingredients, as well as to remove any large impurities from them.

d. _____ are used for straining and/or pureeing foods. The openings in the cone can be sizes from very large to very small and depending on the size of the openings can be made of either perforated metal or a mesh screen.

e. A _____ has a curved blade that is rotated over a disk by a hand-operated crank. Most professional models have interchangeable disks with holes of varying fineness.

f. _____ is a light, fine-mesh gauze frequently use along with or in place of other straining tools, to strain very fine sauces and similar items. It is also used for making sachets.

Written/Short Answer

1. In the professional bakeshop or pastry kitchen, measurements are taken of:

2. There are a number of safe, practical ways to store knives, including:

3. Name five of the tools most commonly used in bread baking:

4. Name six different tools commonly used in décor work:

5. List five tools commonly used in confectionery and décor work:

6. Name three different kinds of mixer found in a commercial bakeshop or pastry kitchen:

7. Name four kinds of ice cream machines commonly found in commercial bakeshops or pastry kitchens:

Essay

1. Name six different kinds of ovens commonly found in commercial bakeshops and pastry kitchens and their basic characteristics.

2. Name the difference between horizontal and vertical batch freezers.

CHAPTER 4

ADVANCED BAKING PRINCIPLES

Chapter Overview
There are dozens of scientific principles at work in baking. As an introduction to the topic of food science, this section provides an overview of the most basic of these principles.

Chapter Objectives
After reading and studying this chapter, you should be able to:
> - Identify the five basic baking ingredients and their two sub-categories.
> - Define what a leavener is and identify the most common products and methods used to leavening baked products.
> - Identify the properties of sweeteners and how they are altered in baked products.
> - Identify the properties of thickeners and how they are altered in baked products.
> - Define an emulsion and describe its properties.
> - Define an overview of the process of tempering chocolate.

Study Outline

Key Terms and Concepts
Baking Science

stabilizers	liquefiers	gluten
gluten-to-starch ratio	primary liquefier	shortening agents

Leaveners

organic leavener	chemical leavening agents	
Saccharomyces cerevisiae	fermentation	alkali
acid	sodium bicarbonate	single-acting
double-acting	mechanical leavening	foaming mixing method
creaming mixing method	lamination	

Sweeteners

monosaccharide	oligosaccharide	fructose
dextrose	disaccharide	sucrose
polysaccharide	crystallization	saturation levels
agitation	seeding	invert sugar
crystalline structore	noncrystalline structure	

Hygroscopic Properties of Sugar and Salt

hygroscopic	caramelization	Maillard reaction

Thickeners

gelatinization
amylopectin
gelatin
coagulation

polysaccharides
retrogradation
bloom
partial-coagulation

amylose
pectin
gel

Emulsions

emulsion

immiscible liquid

temporary emulsion

Tempering Chocolate

cocoa butter
alpha

beta
beta prime

gamma

Self Study Questions

True/False

_____ 1. A general knowledge of how basic ingredients can be changed through the effects of temperature, agitation, and/or acids or alkalis gives the baker or pastry chef the freedom to develop new items.

_____ 2. Wheat is the only grain that forms measurable amounts of gluten, making it an indispensable grain in the kitchen or bakeshop.

_____ 3. A flour with a higher gluten content will result in a much softer crumb, whereas a flour with a lower gluten content will result in a tougher crumb.

_____ 4. Some liquefiers, such as sugar, may actually tighten or bind a dough when first added, but their interaction with other ingredients ultimately tenderizes, or loosens, the dough or batter.

_____ 5. If the total amount of fat added to a dough or batter equals no more than 30% of the weight of the finished dough or product, it acts to increase the elasticity of the proteins in the flour thereby helping the bread or other product expand during baking.

_____ 6. Given the proper environment, yeast cells will continue to ferment until either they run out of food or the by-products of fermentation begin to poison them and they die.

_____ 7. Too much salt can damage or kill yeast cells by dehydrating them.

_____ 8. In leavening with baking soda or baking powder, an alkaline ingredient interacts with an acid. When combined with a liquid, they react to produce carbon dioxide that expands during baking, leavening the dough or batter.

Multiple Choice

1. It is the _____ (the protein component in flour) that builds structure and strength in baked goods
    a. gluten
    b. sugar
    c. starch
    d. viscosity

2. _____ is made from cow's milk and is approximately 80% fat, 10-15% water and 5% milk solids.
    a. Lard
    b. Butter
    c. Oil
    d. Shortening

3. In the _____ eggs, egg yolks, and/or egg whites are beaten to incorporate air until they form a foam.
    a. meringue method
    b. creaming method
    c. lamination method
    d. foaming method

4. The term _____ refers to a sugar (sucrose or table sugar) whose optical or refractory properties have been altered.
    a. invert sugar
    b. retrograde sugar
    c. complex sugar
    d. crystal

Fill in the Blank

1. Gluten is composed of two distinct proteins: _____ and _____.

2. The ideal temperature for fermentation is between _____ and _____.

3. _____ and _____ are two commonly known monosaccharides.

4. The _____ blends fat and sugar together to incorporate air.

5. _____ occurs when egg proteins begin to coagulate and liquid is trapped in the network of set proteins, resulting in a smooth rather thick texture.

Matching

1. Matching: Gelling and/or thickening agents and their sources

Draw lines to match each of the following starches with its source. Note that different starches may be derived from the same type of source. Use all options listed.

Modified food starches	Root
Cornstarch	Various
Flour	Tuber
Arrowroot	Tuber
Tapioca/Cassava	Sea vegetable
Potato	Citrus skins, apples
Agar-Agar	Animal
Pectin	Animal
Gelatin	Grain
Eggs	Grain

Written/Short Answer

1. Four functions of sugar in baking are:

2. Three functions of salt in bread baking.

3. Name five things that influence sugar crystallization.

4. Name three benefits of glucose syrup.

5. Pectin is a carbohydrate derived from the cell walls of certain fruits. Name four of the common sources of pectin:

6. Cocoa butter, the fat found in chocolate, may set into one of four types of crystals. Name these four types of crystals.

Short Answer/Essay

1. Define the two processes that create browning.

2. Define the system known as a "gel."

CHAPTER 5

FOOD AND KITCHEN SAFETY

Chapter Overview
The importance of storing and preparing food properly cannot be overemphasized. In addition to the precautions necessary to guard against food-borne illness, care must also be taken to avoid accidents involving staff or guests. Practicing and monitoring safe procedures will keep both your employees and customers safe from food-borne illness and injury.

Chapter Objectives
After reading and studying this chapter, you should be able to:
- ➤ Discuss food safety and identify ways to prevent food-borne illness in the professional bakeshop and pastry kitchen.
- ➤ Define HACCP and the method of implementing the food safety system into the professional bakeshop and pastry kitchen.
- ➤ Identify kitchen safety measures that when implemented daily reduce the risk of healthy hazards and injury.
- ➤ Discuss a general overview of regulations, inspection and certification that pertain to the professional bakeshop and pastry kitchen.

Study Outline

Key Terms and Concepts
Food Safety & Food-borne Illness
adulterated foods	chemical contaminants	physical contaminants
biological contaminants	pathogen	intoxication
infection	botulism	salmonellosis
E. *coli 0157:H7*	fungi	virus
parasites	*Trichinella spiralis*	bacteria
aerobic bacteria	anaerobic bacteria	facultative bacteria
mesophilic bacteria	thermophilic bacteria	psychrophilic bacteria
fission	endospores	

Keeping Foods Out of the Danger Zone
"First in first out" (FIFO)	cold holding equipment	HACCP
hazard analysis	critical control points (CCP)	critical limits
corrective action plan	time/temperature logs	verification system
cleaning	sanitizing	pests

Kitchen Safety & Regulations, Inspection and Certification
fire safety plan	Ansul system	OSHA
Americans with Disabilities Act		

Basic Methods Overview

Basic Hand Washing

1. Wet hands.
2. Apply soap.
3. Use a nail brush to clean cuticles and under nails.
4. Scrub well for 20 seconds.
5. Rinse hands thoroughly in warm water.
6. Dry hands completely using a disposable (paper) towel.

Thawing Frozen Foods Properly

Thaw slowly under refrigeration:
1. Place food, still wrapped in a shallow container on the bottom shelf until thawed.

Under running water:
1. Covered or wrapped food can be placed in a container under running water approximately 70°F/21°C or below.
2. Use a stream of water strong enough to wash loose particles of ice off the food, but do not allow the water to splash on other food or surfaces.
3. Be sure to clean and sanitize the sink both before and after the thawing.

Microwave:
1. Individual portions that are to be cooked immediately can be thawed in a microwave oven.
Note: Liquids, small items, or individual portions can be cooked without thawing but larger pieces of solid or semisolid foods that are cooked while still frozen become overcooked on the outside before they are thoroughly done throughout.

Hazard Analysis Critical Control Points (HACCP) Food Safety Program

1. Assess the hazards.
2. Identify the critical control points (CCP).
3. Establish critical limits and control measures
4. Establish procedures for monitoring critical control points (CCP).
5. Establish corrective action plans.
6. Set up a record-keeping system.
7. Develop a verification system.

Preventing pest infestation

1. Clean all areas and surfaces thoroughly
2. Wipe up spills immediately and sweep up crumbs.
3. Cover garbage, and remove it every 4 hours.
4. Elevate garbage containers on concrete blocks.
5. Keep food covered or refrigerated
6. Check all incoming boxes for pests and remove boxes as soon as items are unpacked.
7. Store food away from walls and floors, and maintain cool temperatures and good ventilation.
8. Prevents pests from entering the facility by installing screened windows and screened self-closing doors.
9. Fill in all crevices and cracks, repair weak masonry, and screen off any openings to the buildings, including vents, basement windows, and drains.
10. If necessary, consult a professional exterminator.

Working safely

1. Clean up grease and other spills as they occur. Use salt or cornmeal to absorb grease, then clean the area.
2. Warn coworkers when you are coming up behind them with something hot or sharp.
3. Alert the pot washer when pots, pans, and handles are especially hot.
4. Beware of grill fires. If one occurs, do not attempt to put it out with water. Removing excess fat and letting any marinades drain completely from foods to be grilled will help prevent flare-ups.
5. Keep fire extinguishers in proper working order and place them in areas of the kitchen where they are most likely to be needed.
6. Remove lids from pots in such a manner that the steam vents away from your face, to avoid steam burns.
7. Bend at the knees, not the waist, to lift heavy objects.
8. Pick up anything on the floor that might trip someone.
9. Learn about first aid, CPR, and mouth-to-mouth resuscitation. Have well-stocked first-aid kits on hand.
10. Make sure that all dining room and kitchen staff know how to perform the Heimlich maneuver on a choking person. Post instructions in readily visible areas of the kitchen and dining room.
11. Handle equipment carefully, especially knives, mandolines, slicers, grinders, band saws, and other equipment with sharp edges.
12. Observe care and caution when operating mixers. Always keep your hands away from an operating mixer.
13. Use separate cutting boards for cooked and raw foods, and sanitize after using.
14. Wash hands thoroughly after working with raw foods.

15. Use tasting spoons, and use them only once — do not "double-dip." Do not use your fingers or kitchen utensils when tasting food.
16. Store any toxic chemicals (cleaning compounds and pesticides, for example) away from food to avoid cross contamination.
17. Use only dry side towels for handling hot items.
18. Use instant-read thermometers (and sanitize them after using) to ensure that adequate temperatures are reached.
19. Post emergency phone numbers near every phone.

Self Study Questions

Fill in the blank

1. _____ account for the majority of food-borne illnesses.

2. _____ may cause injury as well as illness.

3. The danger zone is between _____ and _____.

4. Foods left in the danger zone for more than _____ hours is considered adulterated.

Multiple-Choice

1. Food is at greatest risk of cross contamination during:
    a. The preparation stage
    b. The cooking stage
    c. The cooling stage
    d. The plating stage

2. Proper hand washing requires using soap and:
    a. 85°F water for 20 seconds
    b. 110°F water for 15 seconds
    c. 120°F water for 30 seconds
    d. 110°F water for 20 seconds

3. To hold hot foods safely, make sure they are above:
    a. 165°F
    b. 140°F
    c. 170°F
    d. 135°F

Short Answer/Essay

1. What is the proper way to reheat foods?

2. What are the seven principles of HACCP?

3. Explain critical limits and control measures for HACCP.

4. What is the difference between cleaning and sanitizing?

5. What is the proper water temperature for a ware-washing machine?

6. Name three ways to avoid pests in your facility.

7. Name three ways to practice fire safety.

8. What is the proper dress for in the kitchen?

CHAPTER 6

BAKING FORMULAS AND BAKERS' PERCENTAGES

Chapter Overview
A baker or pastry chef needs to perform a number of key calculations in order to have consistently successful results and work efficiently. This chapter provides a brief overview of some of the basic mathematical formulas and calculations used in the bakeshop and pastry kitchen to create standardized production formulas, increase or decrease a formula's yield (a technique known as scaling), and adjust to different production needs.

Chapter Objectives
After reading and studying this chapter, you should be able to:
- ➤ Explain how to thoroughly review a formula in preparation for using it as part of baker's *mise en place*.
- ➤ Identify the different base measurements for both weight and volume.
- ➤ Define the term, *standardized formula*.
- ➤ Identify the component parts of standardized formulas and why they are important
- ➤ Define and be able to apply *formula conversion factors*.
- ➤ Explain how to convert to common units of measure.
- ➤ Explain how to convert the number of portions in a formula.
- ➤ Master the conversion of volume to weight and weight to volume.
- ➤ Master conversions between U.S. and Metric measurement systems.
- ➤ Calculate cost per formula unit of measure.
- ➤ Calculate the as-purchased quantity (APQ) and edible portion quantity (EPQ) in a formula.
- ➤ Calculate edible-portion costs (EPC).
- ➤ Master an understanding of bakers' percentages and apply them effectively in formulas.
- ➤ Explain how desired dough temperature (DDT) and the total temperature factor (TTF) affect dough preparation.

Study Outline

Key Terms and Concepts
Baking Formulas and Scaling with Precision

baker's mise en place	count	volume
weight	each	bunch
dozen	volume	teaspoon
tablespoon	fluid ounce	cup
pint	quart	gallon
milliliter	liter	ounce
pound	gram	kilogram

Standardized Formulas

standardized   standardized formula   yield
portion information   ingredient names   ingredient measures
ingredient preparation instructions
equipment information   preparation steps
service information   holding/reheating procedures

Formula Calculations

recipe   formula   conversion
formula conversion factor (FCF)   original yield   desired yield
common unit of measure

Volume Versus Weight Measure & U.S. and Metric Measurement Systems

Celsius   Fahrenheit   kilo
hecto   deka   deci
centi   milli

Calculation Formulas

total cost   number of units   cost per unit
edible-portion quantity (EPQ)   as-purchased quantity (APQ)
edible-portion cost (EPC)   bakers' percentages   percentage value
yield percentage   total temperature factor (TTF)
desired dough temperature (DDT)
friction   British Thermal Units (BTUs)

Self Study Questions

True/False

_____ 1. Ingredients are purchased and used following one of three measuring conventions: count, volume or weight.

_____ 2. Weight is the measurement of space occupied by a solid, liquid or gas.

_____ 3. Unlike published recipes meant to work in a variety of settings for a wide audience, standardized formulas suit the specific needs of an individual pastry kitchen or bakeshop.

_____ 4. Portion information is one of the key elements that should be included in a standardized formula.

_____ 5. Desired yield divided by original yield of a formula equals the formula conversion factor.

_____ 6. It is important to remember that weight is measured in fluid ounces and volume is measured in ounces.

_____ 7. Measuring dry ingredients by weight is much more accurate, and it is the preferred and most common method used for measuring dry ingredients in professional kitchens and bakeshops.

_____ 8. Generally, the as-purchase quantity obtained by the as-purchase quantity formula is rounded up, since the yield percentage is, by nature, an estimate.

_____ 9. In calculating the number of servings from an edible portion quantity, you should always round up if the yield results in a whole number of portions, plus a partial portion.

_____ 10. The real desired dough temperature for enriched dough is slightly higher, as it is important to keep the fats that have been added to the dough soft while it is being worked.

Multiple Choice

1. The common conversion to volume and common unit (U.S.) for 1 gallon is _____ and
_____.
   a. 2 pints, 32 fluid ounces
   b. 8 tablespoons, 16 fluid ounces
   c. 4 quarts, 128 fluid ounces
   d. 2 cups, 16 fluid ounces

2. The term "deka" is the metric prefix for _____.
   a. 10
   b. 1/10
   c. 1/100
   d. 100

3. The U.S. Measurement System uses _____ and _____ to measure weight.
   a. grams and kilograms
   b. tablespoons and teaspoons
   c. ounces and pounds
   d. cups and kilograms

4. The Total Cost divided by the Number of Units = _____.
   a. Edible portion quantity
   b. Number of packs in the unit
   c. Cost per unit
   d. Cost per as-purchased quantity

5. In preparing to calculate the yield of fresh produce, you should save the _____ and
_____ in separate containers.
   a. as-purchased quantity, edible-portion quantity
   b. usable trim, edible-portion quantity
   c. unusable trim, usable trim
   d. as-purchased quantity, unusable trim

Fill in the Blank

1. The following terms _____, _____, and _____ all indicate units of count measure.

2. Standardized formulas can be _____ or _____, using a recipe software management program.

3. The "Equipment Information" included in a standardized formula should advise the user what equipment is needed for _____, _____, _____, and _____.

4. Two pieces of information needed to calculate the Formula conversion Factor are: _____ and _____.

5. To determine the percentage value for each ingredient in a formula, simply divide the: _____ by the _____ and then multiply the result by _____.

Matching

1. Matching: Converting to a Common Unit of Measure

Formula Measure	Common conversion to Volume	Common Unit (U.S.)
1 pound	2 pints	16 ounces
1 tablespoon	N/A	128 fluid ounces
1 cup	4 quarts	16 fluid ounces
1 pint	16 tablespoons	32 fluid ounces
1 quart	2 cups	1/2 fluid ounce
1 gallon	3 teaspoons	8 fluid ounces

Written/Short Answer

1. Name four common terms used to identify weight.

2. Standardized formulas establish four critical elements that allow them to be used easily between one operation and another, one shift and another and one employee and another.

3. Standards established through the application of standardized recipes allow pastry chefs and bakers to do the following things:

4. Three common calculations needed in purchasing and costing formulas are:

5. The two basic functions of bakers' percentages are:

Essay

1. Define the formula for converting Celsius to Fahrenheit.

2. Define the formula for converting Fahrenheit to Celsius.

3. Define the principle of bakers' percentage.

CHAPTER 7

BEGINNER YEAST BREADS AND ROLLS

Chapter Overview

When flour, water, yeast, and salt are worked together in the correct proportions for the appropriate amount of time and at the proper temperature, proper gluten structure develops. The bread baker knows that the ingredients play a key role in the quality of the dough, as do the mixing and fermentation methods. The techniques in this chapter take the bread-baking process up through a finished dough.

Chapter Objectives

After reading and studying this chapter, you should be able to:

➤ Define the stages of mixing bread dough and mixing times and speeds.
➤ Describe how to accurately substitute on type of yeast for another.
➤ Apply the principle of Desired Dough Temperature
➤ Master the technique of bulk fermentation.
➤ Explain how the preparation of fiber-enriched doughs differs from other doughs.
➤ Explain how enriched doughs differ from other doughs.
➤ Explain the importance of scaling and pre-shaping in the preparation of doughs.
➤ Explain the importance of "resting" dough or intermediate fermentation.
➤ Understand the importance of final shaping.
➤ Explain the process of final fermentation.
➤ Master finishing techniques for beginner yeast breads and rolls.
➤ Understand the principles at work when baking yeast-raised doughs.
➤ Identify and master the guidelines for successfully making bagel dough.

Study Outline

Key Terms and Concepts
Direct Fermentation and Stages of Mixing

straight mixing method	pickup period	initial development period
final development period	Direct fermentation	lean dough
Stages of mixing	dough temperature	enriched dough

Yeast

fresh yeast	active dry yeast	instant dry yeast

Desired Dough Temperature and British Thermal Units
Desired Dough Temperature (DDT) ambient temperature
British Thermal Units

Bulk Fermentation

bulk fermentation

relax

carbon dioxide

hydration

gluten strands

folding over

ethyl alcohol

leaven

retarding

food supply

slack dough

bucky

Scaling and Preshaping

boule

preshaping

scaling

bulk fermentation

Resting or Intermediate Fermentation

bench rest

intermediate fermentation

table rest

secondary fermentation

folding over

final shaping

Final Shaping and Finishing Techniques

proofing

washes

scoring

batard

lame

final fermentation

Baking

oven spring

venting time

split loaf

crust and color development   cooling

Yeast-Raised Bread Types

Lean Dough

Grissini

Bagels

Soft Rolls

Pullman

Challah

bâtard

Cider Bread

Pain de mie

Parker House rolls

Beer Bread

Yeast-raised doughnuts

Berliners

Pita

Knot rolls

Durum Dough

Basic Methods Overview

Straight Mixing Method

For this mixing method the ingredients are added in different order depending on the type of yeast used.

1. If instant dry yeast is used the yeast should first blended with the flour and then all other ingredients should be placed in the bowl on top of the flour-yeast mixture. If active dry or compressed fresh yeast is used the yeast should first be blended with the water and allowed it to fully dissolve.

2. Next the flour should be added and all remaining ingredients should be placed on top of the flour.

3. After all the ingredients are in the mixing bowl they should be blended together on low speed until just combined. Then turn the mixer to medium speed and blend the dough to full development.

Stages of Mixing and Mixing Times and Speeds

1. Stage one: Pick-up period

   This stage occurs when the ingredients are blended on low speed until the ingredients are just combined. The dough is a wet, sticky, rough mass at this point.

2. Stage two: Clean-up period, or preliminary development

   At this point the dough is mixing at a moderate speed and will appear somewhat rough.

3. Stage three: Development period

   The elasticity of the gluten begins to develop and the dough begins to pull away from the sides of the mixing bowl. At this point the mixer should also be running at a medium speed. A high speed would work the dough too roughly at this point and begin to break the structure of the gluten, rather than promoting its development.

4. Stage four: Final gluten development

   At this point the dough is smooth and elastic and leaves the sides of the bowl completely clean as the mixer is running. Full gluten development may be tested and determined by removing a piece of dough from the mixer and stretching it. If the dough will stretch to form a thin membrane, which allows light to filter through, then the gluten has been properly and sufficiently developed.

Shaping Large Rounds (from 6 oz to 4 1/2 lb/170 to 2.04 kg):

1. Position the dough so one long edge is parallel to the edge of the work surface.
2. Fold the top edge of the dough down to the bottom edge. Using the heel of your hand, seal the two edges together. Rotate the dough 90 degrees.
3. Fold the top edge of the dough down to the bottom edge. Using the heel of your hand, seal the two edges together.
4. Cup both hands around the dough and pull it toward you until the seam is on the bottom.

Shaping Small Rounds (from 2 to 6 oz/57 to 170 g):

1. Position the dough so one long edge is parallel to the edge of the work surface.
2. Fold the top edge of the dough down to the bottom edge. Using the heel of your hand, seal the two edges together. Rotate the dough 90 degrees.
3. Fold the top edge of the dough down to the bottom edge. Using the heel of your hand, seal the two edges together.
4. Place your hand over the ball of dough and curl your fingers so that the first knuckles of your fingers are touching the table. Your fingertips should almost be touching the palm of your hand, and your thumb should be out to the side and touching the table; the heel of your hand should also be touching the table. The dough should be sitting near the top of your palm, near your thumb, forefinger, and middle finger.
5. Using your palm, push the dough away from you in an arc to the right. Using your fingertips, pull the dough toward you in an arc to the left. Repeat this circular motion, applying gentle pressure while rounding the dough, to create a tight, smooth ball.

Shaping Large Oblongs (from 12 oz to 1 3/4 lb/340 to 794 g):

1. Position the dough so one long edge is parallel to the edge of the work surface.
2. Stretch the dough into a 10-in/25.4-cm-long rectangle. Fold the left and right edges of the rectangle into the center of the dough, pressing the dough lightly with your fingertips.
3. Fold the top edge of the dough down to the center of the dough, pressing lightly with your fingertips. Fold the top of the dough down to the bottom edge. Seal the two edges together, using the heel of your hand.
4. Roll the dough into an even cylinder 6-in/15.25-cm long.

Shaping Small Oblongs (from 3 to 6 oz/85 to 170 g):

1. Turn the dough so one long edge is parallel to the edge of the work surface.
2. Stretch the dough into a 3-in/7.62-cm-wide rectangle. Fold the left and right edges of the rectangle into the center of the dough, pressing the dough lightly with your fingertips.
3. Fold the top edge of the dough down to the center of the dough, pressing lightly with your fingertips. Fold the top of the dough down to the bottom edge. Seal the two edges together, using the heel of your hand.
4. Roll the dough into an even cylinder 3-in/7.62-cm long.

Self Study Questions

True/False

_____ 1. By keeping loaves uncovered during resting or intermediate fermentation, you can prevent a skin from forming.

_____ 2. A boule is reshaped using the same method as for preshaping

_____ 3. Large items, such as loaves, should be proofed to a slightly less developed state than smaller items, as they require longer baking times and will continue to ferment (proof) for a longer time in the oven.

_____ 4. Baking an unscored bread results in an unevenly shaped loaf.

_____ 5. An egg wash acts to gelatinize the starches on the surface of the dough to facilitate crust formation.

_____ 6. The first step in shaping a bâtard is flattening the pre-shaped oblong.

_____ 7. Bagel dough should be mixed just until the ingredients are combined without overmixing.

_____ 8. Doughnuts should be finished while they are still slightly warm.

Multiple Choice

1. Accurate scaling guarantees the correct _____ of the dough pieces when dividing.
   a. weight
   b. texture
   c. smoothness
   d. color

2. Always lay the shaped dough pieces on the bench in _____.
   a. the order they are shaped.
   b. in the verse order that they are shaped
   c. from largest to smallest
   d. from smallest to largest

3. It is necessary for bagel dough to contain_____ and _____.
   a. high gluten flour, glucose syrup
   b. malt syrup, poppyseeds
   c. high gluten flour, malt syrup
   d. low gluten flour, malt syrup

Fill in the Blank

1. Scaling time should not exceed _____ to _____ minutes.

2. The ambient temperature for the final proof should be from _____, to _____ for maximum yeast activity.

3. If the temperature during the final proof is too high, insufficient yeast activity will result in _____, _____, and _____.

4. Some breads, such as _____ are scored with traditional scoring patterns that are used as a way to label the breads, making it easy for both clients and staff to identify them.

5. As dough is baked and reaches an internal temperature of _____, the yeast dies.

Written/Short Answer

1. Three steps in shaping a boule are:

2. During the stage of final fermentation, doughs or shapes may be placed on/in

3. Four of the factors that help determine the amount of time a bread bakes are:

4. Once loaves are baked, it is important that they be cooled properly in order:

Essay

1. Describe the shaping and final preparation of bagel dough.

2. Explain the factors that may affect the temperature at which breads are baked.

40

CHAPTER 8

ADVANCED YEAST BREADS AND ROLLS

Chapter Overview
The way in which yeast is introduced into the dough—by either direct or indirect fermentation—gives the bread baker the range of techniques necessary to create simple lean dough quickly and efficiently and to create hearty breads using such indirect fermentation methods as sponges, polishes, bigas, and sourdough. This chapter examines these more complex methods and presents numerous examples of their use in popular bakes goods.

Chapter Objectives
After reading and studying this chapter, you should be able to:
- ➢ Understand the different preferments and how they are used.
- ➢ Master the technique of indirect fermentation.
- ➢ Master the technique of working with wet doughs.
- ➢ Master a comprehension and application of sour dough starters.
- ➢ Describe how flavorings and garnishes are added to doughs.
- ➢ Master shaping of advanced breads.

Study Outline

Key Terms and Concepts
Indirect Fermentation and Pre-Ferments

pâte fermentée	sponge method	poolish
biga	sourdough	hot soaker
cold soaker	wet dough	primary leavener
lactic acid	acetic acid	culture

Fiber-Enriched Doughs

Autolyse	soakers	folding method

Basic Methods Overview

Biga Preparation and Usage

1. To prepare the biga, combine the flour, water, and yeast. Mix on low speed for 3 minutes, or until thoroughly combined. Transfer to a container, cover, and ferment at room temperature (75ºF/24ºC) for 18 to 24 hours, until the biga has risen and begun to recede; it should still be bubbly and airy.

2. To prepare the final dough, combine the flour and yeast. Add the water, biga, and salt. Mix on low speed for 4 minutes and on medium speed for 1 minute. The dough should be blended but not too elastic (ciabatta is a wet, slack dough).

3. Bulk ferment the dough in a tub or bowl until nearly doubled, about 30 minutes. Fold gently four times in half (the dough should feel like jelly). Ferment for another 30 minutes. Fold again, gently, two times in half. Allow the dough to ferment for another 15 minutes before dividing.

Making a Sourdough Starter:

To begin a culture start with:

1 pt/480 ml of water
1 to 3 lb/454g to 1.36 kg of organic wheat, durum, or rye flour

1. Combine 1 to 3 lb/454 to 1.36 kg of organic wheat, durum, or rye flour and 1 pt/480 ml of water and knead into a uniform dough. (Adjust the amount of flour to produce a stiffer or looser sours], as preferred.)

2. Transfer to a plastic tub large enough to permit the mixture to at least double in volume.

3. Cover with additional flour, cover, and let ferment at room temperature (75°F/24°C) until the sour has risen and is just starting to fall approximately 3 days. It is now ready to use to prepare a sourdough.

Self Study Questions

True/False

_____ 1. The addition of fat and/or sugar does not have a significant impact on the finished bread product.

_____ 2. In working with wet dough, after mixing, it should be transferred directly onto the wooden work surface that has been coated generously with flour.

_____ 3. For wet doughs, the folding step does not require much attention to detail.

_____ 4. The longer the yeast in a dough remains active, the better the flavor and texture of the finished bread.

Multiple Choice

1. _____ means that some portion of the dough is allowed to ferment on its own before being mixed with the remainder of the formula's ingredients.
   a. Sour dough starter
   b. Proofing
   c. Indirect fermentation
   d. Direct fermentation

2. A _____ combines equal parts flour and water (by weight) with some yeast.
   a. poolish
   b. biga
   c. sour dough
   d. pâte fermentée

3. _____ are established by capturing wild yeast in a flour and water dough.
   a. Sponge
   b. Biga
   c. Sour dough
   d. Pâte fermentée

4. To maintain or build up an established sourdough starter, it should be given additional feedings of _____ and _____.
   a. sugar, salt
   b. flour, water
   c. flour, sugar
   d. salt, oil

Fill in the Blank

1. Both _____ and _____ flours are used in sourdough starters.

2. A _____ combines equal parts flour and water.

3. Autolyse is especially useful in _____.

4. A hot soaker _____ the _____ of the soaker's grain.

Matching

1. Matching – Pre-ferments

Pâte fermentée _____
Sponge (method)_____
Poolish _____
Biga _____
Sourdoughs _____

a. _____ combines equal parts flour and water (by weight) with some of yeast (the amount varies according to the expected length of fermentation time, using less for longer, slower fermentations). It is fermented at room temperature long enough to double in volume and start to recede, or decrease in volume. This may take anywhere from 3 to 15 hours. It should be mixed in a plastic or other non-reactive container large enough to hold the mixture comfortably as it ferments.

b. _____ are established by capturing wild yeast in a flour and water dough.

c. _____ or "old dough," is nothing more exotic than a piece of a wheat lean dough reserved from the previous day's production. The dough is covered and refrigerated until needed, then added along with the other ingredients to make a batch of dough. The yeast in this pre-ferment has enjoyed an extended fermentation and will have developed a rich, appealing "sour" flavor.

d. _____ is the stiffest of the pre-ferments. It contains flour and enough water to equal 50 to 60 percent of the flour's weight as well as 0.33 to 0.5 percent of the formula's total yeast. After the pre-ferment has properly fermented, it must be loosened with a portion of the formula's liquid to make it easier to blend into the dough.

e. A _____ combines one-third to one-half of the formula's total flour with all the yeast and enough liquid to make a very loose dough. This pre-ferment can made be made directly in the mixing bowl, as the fermentation period is typically less than 1 hour. When it has doubled in size, the remaining ingredients are mixed in to make the final dough.

Written/Short Answer

1. Name four reasons why dough is folded over?

2. Name two advantages that result from the use of an autolyse.

3. Name four fresh produce items that contain a high percentage of natural yeasts that can be added to a sourdough starter mixture to speed its development process.

Essay

1. Define the term "soaker" and name two ways in which a soaker is prepared?

2. Name the various ways to add garnish to a dough.

CHAPTER 9

PASTRY DOUGHS AND BATTERS

Chapter Overview

Pastry doughs are the foundation for a wide range of preparations. Pie dough, short dough, and puff pastry are only a few examples. All are made of the same basic ingredients, but different preparation techniques give them vastly different characteristics, making each suitable for different applications. Pastry batters such as crêpe batter or pâte à choux also serve as elemental preparations and are used in countless classical desserts and pastries.

Chapter Objectives

After reading and studying this chapter, you should be able to:
- Understand and describe the component parts and common characteristics of rubbed doughs and how they are used.
- Understand and describe the component parts and common characteristics of short doughs and how they are used.
- Understand and describe the component parts and common characteristics of crumb crusts and how they are used.
- Understand the properties of pâte à choux, how it is used and master the technique of making it.
- Describe the properties of strudel dough and how it is applied.
- Understand and describe the component parts and common characteristics of laminated doughs, how they are made and how they are used.
- Describe the difference between the various puff pastry dough preparations and explain the advantages of using each.

Study Outline
Key Terms and Concepts
Rubbed Doughs

flaky	mealy	"baking blind"
basic pie dough	pâte brisée	1-2-3 cookie dough

Short Doughs, Crumb Crusts, Pâte à Choux, Strudel Dough

tender crust	crumbly crust	break
curdle	pâte à choux	phyllo dough

Laminated Doughs

croissant	puff pastry	Danish
roll-in	gluten formation	malleable
lock-in	lamination	three-fold method
envelope method	single-fold method	blitz puff pastry
four-fold method	inverted puff pastry	

Basic Methods Overview

Making a rubbed dough:

1. To make a rubbed dough, first flake the firm cold fat into the flour. This can be done by hand, using your fingertips, or in an electric mixer or a food processor (use the metal blade, not the plastic dough blade).

2. Next, add all the liquid at once to the flour-fat mixture and blend the dough quickly but thoroughly.

3. Turn the dough out onto a lightly floured work surface. Gather and press it together into a disk or flat rectangle.

4. Wrap the dough tightly in plastic wrap and chill it under refrigeration until firm enough to work. The period of rest and cooling before working and rolling is vital to ensure that the fat does not become too soft nor the flour overworked.

Making a short dough:

1. To make a short dough, combine the sugar and butter and mix only until it forms a smooth paste to ensure even blending; do not mix vigorously so that air is incorporated.

2. Add the flour and mix at low speed only until just combined; overmixing will make the dough tough. If the dough appears to be somewhat rough or coarse when it is removed from the mixer, work it gently by hand just until it comes together and shape it into a disk or flat rectangle and wrap tightly in plastic.

3. Refrigerate before using to allow the dough to firm up and the gluten to relax.

Making a pâte à choux:

1. Bring the liquid and fat to a rolling boil, then add the flour all at once. Stir constantly to prevent lumps from forming and continue to cook until the mixture pulls away from the sides of the pan.

2. Transfer the mixture to the bowl of an electric mixer and, using the paddle attachment, mix for a few moments to cool the batter slightly. Add the eggs gradually, in three or four additions, mixing the dough until it is smooth again each time. Scrape the sides and bottom of the bowl as necessary. The dough should have a pearl-like sheen and be firm enough to just hold its shape when piped.

"Lock-Ins" for laminated doughs:

1. *Envelope method*: The dough is rolled into a square, or a rectangle. The roll-in is rolled into a smaller square, or rectangle and placed diagonally in the center of the

dough so that each corner points to the center of a side of the dough square. The corners of the dough are then folded over the fat envelope-style so that they meet in the center.

2. *Single-fold method*: The roll-in is rolled into a rectangle that is half the size of the dough square, or rectangle and placed on one half of the dough, then the other half of the dough is folded over it and the edges are sealed to completely encase the roll-in fat.

a. To administer a two-fold, divide the sheet of dough visually in half, and fold the dough over itself to form two layers. This type of fold doubles the number of layers in the pastry.

3. *Three-fold method*: The fat is rolled into a rectangle that covers two-thirds of the dough. The third of the dough not covered with the roll-in fat is folded over to cover half of the roll-in, or the center of the rectangle and then the remaining side (or third) is folded over that. The edges are then sealed to completely encase the roll-in fat. After the lock-in is complete the dough is turned 90 degrees, rolled out to its original dimensions, the first laminating fold is administered, and the dough is wrapped and refrigerated so the gluten will relax and the fat will chill before it is further manipulated.

a. For a three-fold, divide the sheet of pastry visually into thirds, and fold one of the outer thirds of the dough over the middle third of the pastry. Fold the remaining outer third of the dough over the folded dough. This fold triples the number of layers in the dough each time.

4. *Four-fold method or "Book fold"*: Divide the sheet of pastry visually into quarters, and fold the outer quarters into the middle so that their edges meet. Then fold the dough over as if closing a book. This type of fold quadruples the number of layers in the dough each time.

5. *Inverted puff pastry*: The same rules apply as for all other laminated doughs. For inverted puff pastry, the butter layer, rather than the dough, is the outer layer. The dough is worked less when preparing inverse dough, for a more tender result.

Notes about Roll-In:

1. After the roll-in is added to the dough, subsequent folds are usually either three-fold or four-fold (which is also known as the book fold). Each time, before folding and rolling the dough, brush any excess flour from its surface.

2. When you fold the dough, the corners should squarely meet and the edges should be straight and perfectly aligned.

3. After each fold, the dough should be refrigerated to allow it to relax and the butter to chill; the length of time the dough will need to rest will depend in large part on the temperature of the kitchen.

4. For each fold, the dough is turned 90 degrees from the previous one to ensure that the gluten is stretched equally in all directions.

<u>Storage of laminated dough:</u>

1. To prepare puff pastry and other laminated doughs for freezing, and to ease their use when frozen follow this simple procedure.

2. Roll the dough approximately 1/4-in/6.3-mm thick.

3. If necessary, cut the dough into smaller sheets; sheets the size of a sheet pan (16-in by 48-in) or half sheet pan (16-in by 24-in) are often the most practical.

4. Layer the sheets on a sheet pan, placing a sheet of appropriately sized parchment paper between each one.

5. Wrap the pan tightly in plastic wrap and place in the freezer. (Use the same method for refrigerated storage.)

Self Study Questions

True/False

_____ 1. The characteristic flaky texture of rubbed doughs is developed by adding the water or liquid.

_____ 2. Pastry and all-purpose flours are in general, ideal for the rubbed dough method.

_____ 3. If the dough temperature becomes too warm, the fat may become too soft and absorb into the dough, destroying the layers in the dough.

_____ 4. Graham crackers are the only thing used to make crumb crusts.

_____ 5. For pudding and cream pies, the filling is cooked, then poured into the cooled baked crust, and refrigerated until set.

_____ 6. For cheesecakes the batter is pre-baked and then placed into the cooled crumb crust.

_____ 7. In a laminated dough it is the melting fat which leaves spaces between the fine layers of dough and the steam acts to expand the spaces (or pockets), which are set during baking and result in flaky crisp, layers of pastry.

_____ 8. If there are too few layers in a laminated dough the pastry will not rise.

_____ 9. The temperature of the roll-in used in laminated doughs is very important.

Multiple Choice

1. In making rubbed doughs _____ because of its high protein content, will absorb water quickly and in comparatively great quantities, developing gluten readily and in great amounts.
    a. all-purpose flour
    b. bread flour
    c. cake flour
    d. pastry flour

2. _____ is the most common liquid in rubbed dough formulas.
    a. Water
    b. Juice
    c. Milk
    d. Soda

3. If the butter or shortening is more thoroughly worked into the dough, until the mixture resembles coarse meal, the result will be what is sometimes referred to as _____ dough.
    a. mealy
    b. flaky
    c. laminated
    d. homogenous

4. _____ is the preferred choice for short doughs.
    a. cake flour
    b. pastry flour
    c. bread flour
    d. all-purpose flour

5. To prevent a short dough mixture from breaking or curdling, have the eggs and any other liquid ingredients _____ .
    a. heated to 100°F/38°C
    b. frozen and thawed
    c. under refrigeration until the time of mixing
    d. at room temperature

Fill in the Blank

1. _____ and _____ flour have the proper balance of _____ and _____ with the desired amount of water absorptions and gluten development to produce a dough that is both flaky and tender.

2. Of all the fats _____ will yield the most flavor, but it is difficult to handle because it has a lower melting point than _____ or _____ .

3. Mealy pie doughs have a _____, _____ texture than do flaky pie doughs.

4. Short dough contains a high percentage of fat, which produces a very _____ more _____ crust.

5. Pâte à choux is a cooked batter made by combining _____, _____, _____, and _____ .

Matching

1. Matching – Lock-In

Envelope Method _____
Single-Fold Method _____
Three-Fold Method _____
Four-Fold Method _____
Inverted Puff Pastry _____

a. _____: Here the butter layer, rather than the dough, is the outer layer. The dough is worked less when preparing inverse dough, for a more tender result.

b. _____: Divide the sheet of dough visually in half, and fold the dough over itself to form two layers. This type of fold doubles the number of layers in the pastry.

c. _____: Divide the sheet of pastry visually into quarters, and fold the outer quarters into the middle so that their edges meet. Then fold the dough over as if closing a book. This type of fold quadruples the number of layers in the dough each time.

d. _____: The dough is rolled into a square, or rectangle. The roll-in is rolled into a smaller square, or rectangle, and placed diagonally in the center of the dough so that each corner points to the center of a side of the dough square. The corners of the dough are then folded over the fat so they meet n the center.

e. _____: Divide the sheet of pastry visually into thirds, and fold one of the outer thirds of the dough over the middle third of the pastry. Fold the remaining outer third of the dough over the folded dough. This fold triples the number of layers in the dough each time.

Written/Short Answer

1. In the preparation of pastry doughs, name two factors that have a significant impact on the finished baked good.

2. Flaky pie dough is best for:

3. As with flaky pastry dough, mealy dough should be:

    so the butter or other fat will firm and the gluten will relax before the dough is worked and rolled.

4. Refrigerating short dough before rolling allows:

5. Name the two types of preparations that crumb crusts are typically used for:

6. Name two reasons why a crumb crust is pre-baked.

7. In making a pâte à choux batter, a flour with a higher protein content will develop more gluten strands which results in these two effects:

Essay

1. Discuss how fat affects the flakiness of a rubbed dough. Include details about its form, the size of its pieces, temperature, and how it changes during baking.

2. Why is flaky dough poorly suited for preparations where a crust is pre-baked and allowed to cool before liquid filling is added?

3. Why is egg white sometimes added to a crumb crust?

4. Explain the difference in the final product when water versus milk is used to make pâte à choux.

CHAPTER 10

QUICK BREADS AND CAKES

Chapter Overview
Quick breads and cakes are served as breakfast pastries or simple desserts. They are also "foundation preparations" used for assembled cakes and tortes, including wedding and other special-occasion cakes. The pastry chef uses seven basic mixing methods – blending; creaming; two-stage; cold, warm and separated foaming; and combination – to prepare all of these.

Chapter Objectives
After reading and studying this chapter, you should be able to:
- ➤ Explain the basic principles of quick bread and cake preparation
- ➤ Describe proper pan preparation, cooling and storing techniques for various mixing methods.
- ➤ Define and master the Blending Mixing Method.
- ➤ Define and master the Creaming Mixing Method
- ➤ Define and master the Two-Stage Mixing Method
- ➤ Define and master the Angel Food Mixing Method
- ➤ Define and master Warm and Cold Foaming Methods
- ➤ Define and master the Separated Foam Mixing Method
- ➤ Define and master the Combination Mixing Method
- ➤ Define and master the Chiffon Mixing Method
- ➤ Explain the basic principles cheesecake preparation

Study Outline

Key Terms and Concepts
Basic Principles of Quick Breads and Cakes

chemical leavener	crumb	pan preparation

Mixing Methods

blending mixing method	over-mixing	creaming method
creamed	dense	tender
air incorporation	emulsion	curdled
garnishing ingredients	creaming method	airy
plumping	maceration	rehydration
two-stage mixing method	high-ratio cake	marble
angel food mixing method	chiffon mixing method	ribbon stage
cold foaming method	warm foaming method	meringue
separated foam mixing method	preliminary treatment	fold in

54

combination mixing method   soft peaks

Basic Methods Overview

The Blending Mixing Method:

1. The blending method consists simply of making two mixtures, one with the wet ingredients and one with the dry and then combining the two together.

2. The flour(s) should be sifted together with the other dry ingredients, such as baking soda and/or powder, sugar, salt, cocoa, or ground spices.

3. Solid fats like butter, or shortening, are always melted for this method so they can be blended with the other liquid ingredients.

4. When adding the wet ingredients to the dry ingredients, add them all at once and blend, using a mixer or by hand, just until the dry ingredients are evenly moistened.

5. Scrape the bowl down once or twice to mix the batter evenly. Mixing these batters as briefly as possible ensures a light, delicate texture. Over-mixed batters will develop too much gluten and the resulting item will not have the desired fine, delicate texture.

The Creaming Mixing Method:

1. Cream together the fat and sugar with the paddle attachment on medium speed, scraping down the side and bottom of the bowl occasionally as you work to ensure all the fat is blended evenly until the mixture is pale in color and light and smooth in texture.

2. The eggs should be added gradually and in stages, fully incorporating and scraping down the bowl after each addition.

3. Scraping down the bowl is important to develop a completely smooth batter. Adding the eggs in batches will help to prevent the batter from separating.

4. The sifted dry ingredients are generally added in one of two ways: all at once, or alternating with the liquid ingredient (milk, juice, etc). When adding alternating with a liquid, add one-third of the dry ingredients, then about one-half of the liquid ingredients, mixing until smooth and scraping down the bowl after each addition. Repeat this sequence until all of the dry and liquid ingredients have been added.

5. Increase the speed and beat the batter just until it is evenly blended and smooth. Regardless of the method of addition, after adding the dry ingredients the dough or batter should be mixed minimally, or just until incorporated.

6. The liquid ingredients are also commonly added at one of two places; alternating with the dry ingredients or all at once after the dry ingredients are combined.

7. Lastly add any remaining flavoring or garnishing ingredients such as nuts, chocolate chips, or dried fruit mixing or folding until just incorporated.

The Two-Stage Mixing Method:

1. The first step in this method is to combine, or sift together all the dry ingredients

2. Combine all the wet ingredients, including the eggs.

3. In the first stage, combine the dry ingredient mixture with all of the fat and half of the liquid mixture and mix for 4 minutes on medium speed, scraping down the bowl periodically to ensure the batter is mixed evenly.

4. In the second stage, blend the remaining liquid into the batter in three equal parts, mixing for 2 minutes after each addition, for a total of 6 minutes. Scrape the bowl periodically to make certain that the batter is blended evenly.

Angel Food Mixing Method:

1. For this method, it is important to assemble all equipment and ingredients, and sift the flour and sugar before beginning to mix.

2. After all advance preparation is done, beat the whites until they form soft peaks.

3. Continue whipping and add the sugar, streaming it in gradually with the machine running. Once the meringue has medium, glossy peaks, fold in the sifted dry ingredients by hand, working quickly to reduce the deflation of the beaten egg whites.

4. Sprinkling the tube pan with a small amount of water before adding the batter will help develop a thin crisp crust on the cake.

Cold Foaming Method:

1. Place the eggs and sugar into the bowl of an electric mixer, which will accommodate the volume of the fully beaten eggs.

2. Using the wire whip attachment whip the mixture to maximum volume on high speed. To determine the eggs have reached maximum volume watch as they are

beating and when the aerated mixture just begins to recede, maximum volume has been achieved.

3. At this time remove the bowl from the mixer.

4. Fold the sifted dry ingredients into the beaten eggs; gently and gradually, but quickly to prevent excessive loss of volume. For folding, use a large spatula or other implement, which has a large broad, flat surface.

5. Fold the melted fat into the batter last.

    You may want to temper in the butter, as some chefs feel this will ease its full incorporation and lessen any deflating effects on the batter. To do this first lighten the butter by incorporating a small amount of batter. Then fold this mixture in to the remaining batter.

6. Immediately after mixing, scale off the batter into each prepared pan and bake.

Warm Foaming Method:

1. Place the eggs and sugar in the bowl of an electric mixer, but before beating place the bowl over a pan of barely simmering water and stir the mixture with a wire whip, until it reaches 110°F/43°C.

    Heating the eggs with the sugar before beating causes the mixture to achieve maximum volume faster and creates a more stable foam because the sugar has been dissolved.

2. After egg mixture has reached maximum volume reduce the mixer to medium speed and continue to blend for 5 additional minutes.

3. Fold the sifted dry ingredients into the beaten eggs; gently and gradually, but quickly to prevent excessive loss of volume. For folding, use a large spatula or other implement, which has a large broad, flat surface.

4. Fold the melted fat into the batter last.

5. You may want to temper in the butter, as some chefs feel this will ease its full incorporation and lessen any deflating effects on the batter. To do this first lighten the butter by incorporating a small amount of batter. Then fold this mixture in to the remaining batter.

6. Immediately after mixing, scale off the batter into each prepared pan and bake.

Separated Foam Mixing Method:

1. First, whip the egg yolks with a portion of the sugar to the "ribbon stage", or until the mixture has thickened enough to fall in ribbons from the whip and is pale yellow in color. Set this foam aside.

2. Next, whip the whites until soft peaks form.

3. Gradually add the remaining sugar, with the mixer on medium speed, and continue whipping on medium or high speed until the whites form medium peaks.

4. Immediately after the whites reach their desired peak they should be gently folded into the foamed egg yolks. To fully blend these two components first combine a small measure of the whites with the yolks to lighten them and make their consistency more akin to that of the whites.

5. Fold the remaining whites into the yolk mixture.

6. Fold the remaining ingredients as in the cold and warm foaming methods.

   Fold about one-third of the whites into the yolks to lighten them. Gently but thoroughly fold in the remaining whites until the batter is smooth and there are no visible pockets of egg whites.

   Fold the sifted dry ingredients into the beaten egg mixture; gently and gradually, but quickly to prevent excessive loss of volume.

   For folding, use a large spatula or other implement, which has a large broad, flat surface.

7. Fold the melted fat into the batter last. Immediately after mixing, scale off the batter into each prepared pan and bake.

Combination Mixing Method:

1. The first step in the combination mixing method, after all advance preparation is done is the same as that for a creamed batter: The butter and some of the sugar are creamed together.

2. Whole eggs and yolks from the formula are blended into the mixture.

3. Next, beat the egg whites until soft peaks form and then stream in the sugar gradually with the mixer running on medium speed and beat the whites until medium peaks form.

4. To blend these two mixtures successfully, without deflating the meringue, first add a portion (approximately 1/3) of the meringue to the creamed batter and

blend, this will serve to lighten the dense creamed batter making it able to more easily accept the remaining beaten egg whites. Gently fold in the remaining meringue.

5. Lastly, working gently, but quickly, fold in the sifted dry ingredients and any garnish, such as chopped nuts. It is important to fold the dry ingredients in last.

Chiffon Mixing Method:

1. First sift together the dry ingredients and mix in a portion of the sugar.

2. Blend all the wet ingredients together, except for the egg whites.

3. Next, blend the sifted dry ingredients into the egg yolk mixture.

4. Finally, beat the egg whites until soft peaks form then stream in the remaining sugar gradually with the mixer running on medium speed. Continue beating the egg whites until medium peaks form.

5. Finally, fold the beaten egg whites into the batter. To do this, first lighten the batter by incorporating approximately 1/3rd of the egg whites. Then gently fold in the remaining 2/3 of the beaten egg whites.

Self Study Questions

True/False

_____ 1. Pans are lined with parchment to ease the process of removing a baked product from the pan.

_____ 2. Angel food cakes should have no treatment to the bottom of the pans, as they are cooled upside down to facilitate removal and to help retain their height and inner structure after cooling.

_____ 3. After removal from the oven, quick breads and cakes should be allowed to cool completely in the pan before unmolding.

_____ 4. Items must be cooled completely before they are filled, iced, glazed or otherwise decorated.

_____ 5. In the blending mixing method, solid fats like butter or shortening are most often melted for this method so they can be blended with the other liquid ingredients.

_____ 6. Muffins, cakes, quick breads, cookies, and other baked goods made with the creaming method develop their light and airy structure through the use of mechanical leaveners.

_____ 7. For the creaming method, first the fat and the flour are blended.

_____8. Blending eggs into a butter/sugar mixture creates an emulsion.

_____ 9. Sometimes, but not often, the liquid may be added to the creamed mixture immediately after the eggs.

Multiple Choice

1. All ingredients should be _____ before they are combined.
    a. at room temperature
    b. chilled
    c. frozen
    d. placed in separate bowls

2. Pans should be filled approximately _____ full with batter unless otherwise specified in the formula.
    a. one-half
    b. seven-eighths
    c. one-quarter
    d. three-quarters

3. When dried fruit is added to a formula, whether plumped or not, it is oftenfirst tossed in a small measure of_____, which will help prevent the fruit from sinking to the bottom of the pan during baking.
    a. oil
    b. egg white
    c. flour
    d. batter

4. Angel food cakes have good structure, but because they contain no fat, they have a unique texture which makes them _____ for use in layer cakes or as a component of any layered, sliced dessert or pastry.
    a. less desirable
    b. more desirable

5. After advance preparation is done for an angel food cake, beat the egg whites until they form_____.
    a. stiff peaks
    b. medium peaks
    c. soft peaks

Fill in the Blank

1. Mixing batters made by the blending mixing method as briefly as possible ensures a _____, _____ texture.

2. The first stage of the creaming method involves creaming together the ____ and _____ with the _____ attachment on _____ speed.

3. A high ratio cake is one in which the weight of the _____ is equal to or greater than the weight of the _____ and the weight of the _____ is equal to or greater than the weight of the _____.

4. The two-stage mixing method relies in part on _____ and _____ mixing times than those used in other mixing methods to develop flavor.

5. Angel food cake is a light, spongy cake based on beaten _____ and _____ that is stabilized with _____.

Matching

1. Matching – Batters and Mixing Methods

Lemon Poppy Seed Muffins
Cream Scones
High-Ratio White Cake
Flourless Chocolate Cake
Roulade
Patterned Joconde Sponge

Warm Foaming Method
Blending Mixing Method
Separated Foam Mixing Method
Two-Stage Mixing Method
Combination Mixing Method
Creaming Method

Written/Short Answer
1. Regardless of the method of development and incorporation, air cells facilitate what three things during baking?

2. Pans filled with batters made by what three methods, should be gently tapped on a counter to help to remove any large air bubbles that may have developed as the batter was scaled into the pan.

3. Name some examples of ingredients that should be recognized as contributing moisture to a formula.

4. Name four baked products that typically used the creaming mixing method.

5. To help emulsify or blend a mixture when an unusually large amount of eggs are being added, eggs should be:

6. In the creaming mixing method, name the two ways that the sifted dry ingredients are added:

7. In preparing for the angel food mixing method name the three things you do before beginning to mix.

Essay

1. Why would you apply a thin film of butter or fat to a pan before lining it with parchment in spreading creamed batter thin?

2. Describe the process of unmolding a cheesecake.

3. Briefly define the two-stage mixing method.

CHAPTER 11

COOKIES

Chapter Overview
The word *cookie* derived from a Dutch word that means "small cake." Using this as the contemporary definition, the term *cookie* can include anything from the classic chocolate chunk to twice-baked biscotti to glazed and filigreed petits fours. Each type of cookie requires different shaping techniques such as rolling, stamping, and molding. Many are filled, glazed or otherwise finished after baking.

Chapter Objectives
After reading and studying this chapter, you should be able to:
 ➤ Identify the characteristics of drop cookies and master the technique of making them.
 ➤ Explain the basic principles of pan preparation and cooling for cookies.
 ➤ Identify the characteristics of bar cookies and master the technique of making them.
 ➤ Identify the characteristics of traditional rolled and cut-out cookies and master the technique of making them.
 ➤ Identify the characteristics of stenciled cookies and master the technique of making them.
 ➤ Identify the characteristics of molded cookies and master the technique of making them.
 ➤ Identify the characteristics of twice-baked cookies and master the technique of making them.
 ➤ Identify the characteristics of piped cookies and master the technique of making them.
 ➤ Identify the component parts of glazed petits fours and master the technique of making them.

Study Outline

Key Terms and Concepts
General Pan Preparation and General Cooling Instructions for Cookies
spread   silicone mats   double-panning

Cookie Varieties
drop cookies   bar cookies   traditional rolled cookies
cut-out cookies   stenciled cookies   molded cookies
twice-baked cookies   piping cookies   petits fours

General Terminology

stencils	"tuile" shape	stamped cookies
pressed cookies	springerle	mignardises
frangipane		

Basic Methods Overview

Portioning Drop Cookies:

1. To portion drop cookies using a scoop, fill a scoop of the appropriate size and level it off, then release it onto the parchment lined sheet pan.

2. To portion cookies by slicing, scale the dough into manageable portions and shape each one into a log. Wrap the dough in parchment paper or plastic wrap, using it to compress the dough into a compact cylinder, and refrigerate or freeze until firm. Slice the dough into uniform slices.

Bar Cookies:

1. Bar cookies are baked in large sheets and portioned after baking.

2. If bars are to be glazed or iced, allow the sheet to cool completely before adding the glaze or icing.

3. To ensure clean straight cuts, especially when working with glazed or iced cookies, chill the full sheet before cutting it and dip the knife in warm water and wipe clean before each cut.

Traditional Rolled and Cut-Out Cookies:

1. Cookie dough that is to be rolled and cut should usually be refrigerated to allow the dough to firm up.

2. Line the sheet pans, or prepare them as otherwise directed, before beginning to roll out the dough, so that the cut cookies can be transferred directly to a pan.

3. Divide the dough into manageable portions. Work with one portion at a time, keeping the remainder tightly wrapped and refrigerated.

4. Lightly dust the work surface with flour.

   Some doughs are particularly soft and delicate and should instead be rolled between two sheets of parchment paper.

Generally cookie doughs should be rolled 1/8 to 1/16 inch thick, but the precise thickness depends on the formula.

Stenciled Cookies:

1. Place the stencil on the prepared pan and use a small offset metal spatula to spread a thin, even layer of batter over it; it is important to spread the batter evenly so the cookies bake uniformly.

2. Lift off the stencil, and repeat.

Twice-Baked Cookies:

1. Twice-baked cookies may be prepared by the creaming or foaming methods

2. They are piped or formed into logs or loaves and baked until the internal structure is fully set but the color is not fully developed.

3. Generally the logs are allowed to cool briefly but not completely, so they won't be too brittle when sliced. A serrated blade is less likely to chip and fray the edges of the cookies as they are sliced.

4. The cookies are then further baked at a lower temperature to dry them fully and develop more flavor and color; any seeds and nuts will toast at this point, and the sugars in the dough will caramelize.

Piped Cookies:

1. For piped cookie batters or doughs made with meringue or beaten egg whites, it's especially important to have the pans prepared and the piping bag and pastry tip assembled before mixing the batter.

2. To fill a piping bag with batter, fold the top of the bag down to make a cuff, and use a rubber spatula to fill the bag. Twist the top of the bag to seal and squeeze to release any air in the tip of the bag.

3. To pipe, use constant, even pressure. To finish each cookie, release the pressure and then lift the tip away; if the tip is lifted away before the pressure is released, the batter or dough will form a "tail" at the top of the cookie, which is likely to become dark or burn during baking.

Glazed Petits Fours:

1. The cake it must first be chilled before un-molding, cutting or assembly of the petits fours begins.

2. After the cake has cooled, invert it onto a rack and remove the parchment.

3. Cut the cake crosswise into 3 equal pieces. Spread the top of the first layer with a very thin coating of apricot jam (each finished petit four should be no higher than 1 inch).

4. Top with second layer of cake putting the top of the cake down, spread with jam, and top with the third layer. Spread the last layer with a very thin coating of jam.

5. Roll out 8 oz/227 g of marzipan to 1/8 in/4 mm thickness and cover the top of frangipane. Trim off any excess marzipan and invert the layered cake onto a parchment-lined sheet pan, so the marzipan is on the bottom.

6. Tightly wrap the layered sheet in plastic wrap and refrigerate or freeze until firm. Cut the petits fours into rectangles, squares, or diamonds with a knife or into a variety of shapes (circles, ovals, flowers, etc.) using different cutters.

7. To dip and glaze the cut petits fours, heat and thin the fondant in a bowl that is deep enough to accommodate the petits fours. One at a time, place a petit four upside down in the fondant and gently press it down until the bottom of the cake is level with the surface of the fondant.

8. Remove the glazed cake using two forks (one at the top and one at the base) and place it on an icing screen to allow the fondant to set complete before adding any décor.

9. The classical décor for glazed petit fours is piped filigree, but there are other contemporary décor options; see page 904.

Self Study Questions

True/False

_____ 1. For most drop cookies the upper surface should still look moist but not wet when it is properly baked.

_____ 2. Pan preparation usually includes lining with parchment or silicone baking mats.

_____ 3. Flouring pans as part of pan preparation is commonly recommended.

_____ 4. Some cookies that are too soft to be removed immediately from the pan, should be allowed to cool briefly on the baking pan just until they have set enough to be transferred.

_____ 5. If bar cookies are to be glazed or iced, allow the sheet to cool completely before adding the glaze or icing.

_____ 6. In making bar cookies, it is not critical to ensure that the batter is spread evenly, because it will even out during baking.

_____ 7. Cookie dough that is to be rolled and cut, should usually be refrigerated first.

_____ 8. When using cutters of varying sizes and shapes, bake cookies of like sizes together to ensure even baking.

_____ 9. Stenciled cookies should be baked in large batches, because they require additional effort.

_____ 10. Drying springerle allows a crust to form on the top surface of the cookies, which will preserve the impression during baking by preventing the surface from rising or cracking.

Multiple Choice

1. _____ are made using batters that can be spread and baked without spreading.
    a. Rolled cookies
    b. Cut out cookies
    c. Stenciled cookies
    d. Drop cookies

2. _____ may be formed by hand, stamped, pressed or piped into carved or cast molds to create an intricate design.
    a. Molded cookies
    b. Cut-out cookies
    c. Drop cookies
    d. Stenciled cookies

3. The doughs for _____ cookies are generally prepared by the creaming or foaming methods.
    a. twice-baked
    b. drop
    c. stenciled
    d. cut-out

4. During the second round of baking, twice-baked cookies are further baked at (a) _____ temperature, as the first baking.
    a. higher
    b. the same
    c. lower

5. For _____ made with meringue, it is especially important to have pans prepared and have piping tip and pastry bag ready.
    a. piped batter
    b. drop batter
    c. cut-out dough
    d. stenciled batter

Fill in the Blank

1. When rolling and cutting cookies, the dough will _____ as it is rolled and cut; cut cookies should be quickly _____ to prepared pans so that they do not become _____.

2. In making stenciled cookies, place the _____ on the _____ and use a small, offset, metal _____ to spread a thin, even layer of batter over it.

3. Drying springerle allows a _____ to form on the top surface of the cookies which will preserve the _____ during baking by preventing the surface from _____ and _____.

4. Cookie dough that is to be molded must be _____ enough to hold its _____.

5. Doughs for twice-baked cookies are generally prepared by the _____ or _____ methods.

Matching

1. Matching: Cookies
Match the following cookies with their category.

Springerle	Rolled/Cut Cookies
Pecan Diamonds	Stenciled Cookies
Citrus Crisps	Drop Cookies
Lace Nut Tuiles	Drop Cookies
Chocolate Chunk Cookies	Molded Cookies
Oatmeal Raisin Cookies	Bar Cookies

Written/Short Answer

1. To shape stenciled cookies, they may be:

2. Twice-baked cookies are first piped or formed into logs or loaves and baked until:

3. Name two essential preparation steps when making a piped cookie batter that contains a meringue.

4. Name three commonly known drop cookies:

5. List five major categories by which cookies are classified:

Essay

1. Explain briefly how to portion dough by the slicing method.

2. Describe an alternative method of pan preparation if silicone baking mats are not available when making stenciled cookies.

3. Briefly explain how to properly fill a piping bag with batter.

CHAPTER 12

CUSTARDS, CREAMS, MOUSSES, AND SOUFFLÉS

Chapter Overview
When the pastry chef combines eggs, milk, and sugar and bakes them, the result may be a smooth and creamy crème brûlée or a silky crème caramel. When these same ingredients are stirred together over gentle heat, vanilla sauce, or crème anglaise, is the result. Starches or gelatin can be included to produce textures that range from thick but spoonable to a sliceable cream. Folding in meringue or whipped cream produces mousse, Bavarian cream, diplomat cream, chibouste, or a soufflé.

Chapter Objectives
After reading and studying this chapter, you should be able to:
- ➢ Describe the preparation method for a baked custard
- ➢ Explain the importance of a water bath
- ➢ Unmold a baked custard
- ➢ Caramelize sugar using the dry method
- ➢ Prepare a stirred cream and or pudding
- ➢ Define gelatin and describe its key functions as a thickening agent
- ➢ Prepare a steamed pudding
- ➢ Produce a mousse
- ➢ Prepare a hot soufflé

Study Outline

Key Terms and Concepts
Baked Custards

Cold method	Warm method	Hot water bath

Stirred Creams and Puddings

Gelatin

Stabilizer	Rehydrate	Bloom

Steamed Puddings

Mousse

Aerator	Base	Folding

Bavarian Cream

Hot Soufflés

Self Study Questions

True/False

_____ 1. Milk or cream is the most common liquid used for making custards.

_____ 2. Egg yolks provide a custard with more structure.

_____ 3. The cold method is the best method for making custard.

_____ 4. Crème caramel should not be refrigerated before service.

_____ 5. A hot water bath ensures and even baking temperature.

Multiple Choice

1. A simple baked custard consists of:
   a. egg yolks, cream, and gelatin
   b. eggs, milk or cream and sugar
   c. egg whites, vanilla and cream
   d. eggs and sugar

2. To make a custard by the cold method you
   a. Stir all the ingredients together, pour the mixture into molds and bake.
   b. Bring the cream and the sugar to a boil, add the egg yolks, chill over an ice bath and bake.
   c. Bring all of the ingredients to a boil, pour the mixture into molds and bake
   d. Mix the egg yolks and cream, bake, and chill before adding the sugar and flavorings.

3. A pan to be used for the hot water bath for baking custards should
   a. have sides at least as high as the sides of the molds.
   b. have sides that are half of the sides of the molds.
   c. be as shallow as possible.
   d. a hot water bath is not necessary when baking a custard.

4. _____ is an example of a stirred pudding.
   a. Bread pudding
   b. Yorkshire pudding
   c. Vanilla pudding
   d. Chocolate pudding
   e. Both c and d

Fill in the blank

1. _____ is an example of a soft cheese.

2. Removing custards from a hot water bath after they are removed from the oven will _____ the cooking process.

3. Stirred puddings and creams both contain _____, _____ and a _____.

Matching

1. Hot water bath _____

2. Bloom _____

3. Pastry cream _____

4. Steamed pudding _____

5. Bread pudding _____

    a. A traditional baked custard.
    b. Cake-like in texture, these puddings are unlike others in that they contain very little dairy.
    c. Bain-marie
    d. Uses starch as its main thickening agent
    e. To rehydrate gelatin

Written/Short Answer

1. List the steps for unmolding a baked custard?

2. Why is it important to use a water bath when baking custards?

CHAPTER 13

ICINGS, GLAZES, AND SAUCES

Chapter Overview
The use of an icing, glaze or sauce can mean the difference between a plain baked item and a more elaborate pastry or dessert. These preparations have a wide range of uses, limited only by the imagination of the pastry chef or baker. The techniques and applications involved in making and using them are important to master, as they act to balance and adjust flavors and textures, making them an integral part of any pastry or dessert with which they are paired.

Chapter Objectives
After reading and studying this chapter, you should be able to:
➢ Make a common meringue
➢ Describe the stages of meringues
➢ Prepare different types of buttercream icing
➢ Explain the process of whipping cream
➢ Master the technique of a hard and soft ganache
➢ Describe how to prepare fondant for glazing
➢ Define the different applications for glazes
➢ Produce a vanilla sauce
➢ Prepare a fruit coulis and or sauce

Study Outline

Key Terms and Concepts
Meringue

Common Meringue	Swiss Meringue	Italian Meringue
Soft peak	Medium Peak	Stiff peak

Buttercream

Italian buttercream	German buttercream	French buttercream

Whipping Cream
Fat content

Fondant

Using and Choosing a Sauce

sabayon	chocolate sauce

Fruit sauce   caramel sauce   reduction sauce

Self Study Questions

True/False

_____ 1. Meringues are commonly used for toppings and fillings cakes and pastries.

_____ 2. German buttercream has a long and indefinite shelf life.

_____ 3. The two conditions that should be considered when whipping cream are temperature and fat content.

_____ 4. When whipping cream the cream should be warm or hot.

_____ 5. Fondant is the traditional glaze for petits fours, éclairs and doughnuts.

_____ 6. Avoid serving a dessert with a sauce of the same consistency and texture.

_____ 7. Another term for vanilla sauce is creme anglaise.

_____ 8. The two basic types of caramel sauce are thin and thick.

_____ 9. Reduction sauces are prepared by simmering juices, wines and other alcoholic beverages.

Multiple Choice

1. A meringue is prepared by
     a. whipping egg yolks and sugar
     b. whipping egg whites and sugar
     c. boiling whole eggs and cream
     d. none of the above

2. German buttercream is a combination of
     a. meringue, egg yolks and sugar
     b. pastry cream and honey
     c. pastry cream, butter and flavorings
     d. butter and sugar

3. Glazes should always be
     a. lumpy and hard
     b. applied when cold
     c. smooth, fluid and free of lumps
     d. whipped before use

4. In the traditional Italian preparation of a sabayon what kind of wine is used?
    a. Chardonnay
    b. Marsala
    c. Dry Sherry
    d. Blush

Fill in the Blank

1. The desired temperature of a Swiss meringue is at least _____.

2. All meringues should be _____ and _____.

3. Italian buttercream is made with _____, _____ and _____.

4. Cream for whipping must contain at least _____ % of fat.

5. Before starting any type of sauces you must first prepare an _____.

Matching
1. Meringue _____
2. French buttercream _____
3. Stabilized whipped cream _____
4. Fondant _____
5. Marsala _____
6. Fruit sauces _____

    a. an aerated mixture of egg whites and sugar
    b. made with egg yolks, butter, cooked sugar and flavorings
    c. can be used as a base for flourless soufflés
    d. traditional wine used for a zabaglione
    e. whipped cream with the addition of gelatin
    f. should be heated to 105 F for use

Written/ Short Answer
1. What are the three types of meringue?

2. List and describe the four types of buttercream.

3. How do you prepare a sabayon?

CHAPTER 14

FROZEN DESSERTS

Chapter Overview
Sugar syrups, dairy and custard mixtures, and fruits purées may all be used as the base to make frozen desserts. Any of these bases may then be churn- or still-frozen. These two methods of production yield frozen desserts with vastly different textures. Understanding the principles of each type of frozen dessert will give the chef creative freedom to explore different possibilities of flavor, texture, and presentation.

Chapter Objectives
After reading and studying this chapter, you should be able to:
- Define churn-frozen ice cream.
- Describe how ingredients affect texture and consistency of frozen desserts.
- Explain how to variegate ice cream
- Define gelato and describe how it is different from ice cream.
- Explain the difference between sherbet and sorbet.
- Understand the importance of sugar content in frozen desserts.
- Define granita.
- Understand the techniques of molded and still-frozen desserts.

Study Outline

Key Terms and Concepts
Churn-Frozen ice cream

Overrun	Custard ice cream	Aging	Variegated

Gelato

Gelato	Air incorporation

Sorbet and Sherbet

Sorbet	Sherbet	Stabilizer
Sugar Content	Baumé	Brix
Refractometer		

Granita

Granita	Freezing process

Molded Frozen Desserts
Molding/Un-molding procedures

Still-Frozen Desserts

Pate a bombe	Frozen soufflés	Parfaits

Self Study Questions

True/False

_____ 1. Ice cream can be made only with heavy cream.
_____ 2. It is good to age an ice cream base under refrigeration for several hours before freezing.
_____ 3. Granitas contain more sugar than sorbet.
_____ 4. Molded frozen desserts should not be frozen solid before unmolding.
_____ 5. Gelato has a shorter churning time which results in less air incorporation.
_____ 6. A frozen chocolate soufflé is an example of a still-frozen dessert.

Multiple Choice
1. Custard ice cream contains
    a. crème brulee
    b. gelatin
    c. eggs
    d. cornstarch

2. Too much _____ will diminish the flavor of an ice cream.
    a. heavy cream
    b. overrun
    c. vanilla
    d. aging

3. A good rule for the amount of an ingredient to use for variegation is approximately
    a. 50 percent
    b. 20 percent
    c. 4 percent
    d. 75 percent

4. If there is too much sugar in a sorbet it will
    a. not freeze
    b. develop large crystals
    c. not melt
    d. have a dense texture

5. Gelato tends to be _____ than ice cream.
    a. lighter
    b. higher in overrun
    c. denser
    d. less dense

Fill in the Blank

1. Flavorings such as tea, coffee and spices may be _____ into the cream or milk to make ice cream.

2. Compounds such as praline paste will not affect the _____ of the ice cream.

3. A granita is based on _____, _____, and _____.

4. The sugar density of a sorbet may be checked with a _____ or a _____.

5. The three types of still-frozen desserts are _____, _____, and _____.

6. When using a pulpy fruit purée to flavor an ice cream, _____ the mixture before freezing will create a better emulsion.

Written/Short Answer

1. Describe the procedure for testing the sugar density of a solution to be made into either a sherbet or sorbet.

2. What are the two methods for making frozen desserts?

CHAPTER 15

PIES, TARTS, AND FRUIT DESSERTS

Chapter Overview
Desserts and pastries such as pies, tarts, strudel, and cobblers give the pastry chef or baker the opportunity to showcase the natural, vibrant flavors of fruits and nuts as well as the sweetness and texture of cheeses and dairy products used to make creams and custards. When creating desserts of this type, think of what spices and preparation techniques will enhance and complement the textures, shapes, and flavors of these ingredients.

Chapter Objectives
After reading and studying this chapter the student should be able to:
- ➢ Master the technique of rolling dough and lining a pie or tart pan
- ➢ Explain how to choose a pie or tart filling
- ➢ Produce pies and tarts using the different methods for filling.
- ➢ Describe blind baking and how it applies to the chapter
- ➢ Produce desserts with puff pastry
- ➢ Prepare and use fresh fruit in a dessert
- ➢ Explain the difference between a pie, cobbler, crisp and tart
- ➢ Master the technique of making a traditional strudel

Study Outline
Key Terms and Concepts
Rolling out dough and lining a pie or tart pan

Dusting	Lifting and turning	Docking

Topping pies and tarts

Steam vents	Crumb topping	Pastry top
Lattice	Crimping	Wash

Blind baking pie and tart shells

Pie weights	Coating a prebaked pastry shell

Working with puff pastry

Manageable batches	Baking at high temperature

Working with fresh fruit

Cutting and peeling fresh fruit	High and low moisture fruits
Pitting and coring fruit	Citrus suprêmes

Strudel
Vent   Stretching the dough

Self Study Questions

True/False

_____ 1. Make sure a dough is room temperature before rolling.

_____ 2. Dough for pies and tarts should be rolled to a thickness of 2 inches.

_____ 3. Docking the dough prevents it from bubbling up.

_____ 4. Crumb toppings create more of a moisture barrier.

Multiple Choice

1. The purpose of a wash is to
    a. promote the development of a golden crust
    b. seal in excess moisture
    c. enhance flavor
    d. none of the above

2. The following items can be used to blind bake a pie shell
    a. dry beans
    b. pie weights
    c. both a and b
    d. nuts

3. When baking puff pastry, the temperature of the oven should be high because
    a. to create enough steam to encourage a full rise.
    b. puff pastry is not baked
    c. the dough would stick to the pan at a low temperature
    d. none of the above

4. It is best to peel a kiwi with what utensil?
    a. a paring knife
    b. a vegetable peeler
    c. a teaspoon
    d. a filet knife

Fill in the Blank

1. When working with puff pastry, the dough should be kept as _____ as possible.

2. Blind baking means to bake an _____ pie or tart shell partially or fully _____ adding the filling.

3. A wash for a pastry dough topping could be anything from _____ or _____ to an _____.

Written/Short Answer

1. Highlight the key steps for rolling out dough.

2. Why is strudel dough brushed with butter and rolled?

CHAPTER 16

FILLED AND ASSEMBLED CAKES AND TORTES

Chapter Overview

When selecting components to build a cake or torte, it is important to consider the combination of flavors and textures. Classic cakes and tortes are fine examples of flavor combinations and appealing designs and offer a foundation of inspiration for contemporary applications. Contemporary cakes and tortes explore new flavor combinations generated from the globalization of cuisine and culture.

Chapter Objectives

After reading this chapter the student will be able to:
- ➢ Master the basic assembly of cakes
- ➢ Explain the functions of a garnish
- ➢ Prepare molded cakes
- ➢ Master icing a cake
- ➢ Prepare a gelatin-based filling
- ➢ Master the basic assembly of a traditional layer cake
- ➢ Master glazing a cake
- ➢ Prepare cakes rolled icing (i.e. fondant and marzipan)

Study Outline
Key Terms and Concepts

Basics of cake assembly

Complement	Contrast	Texture
Cake decorating turntable	Simple syrup	

Functions of a garnish

Visual appeal	Flavor/ingredient indicator
Tradition	Decorating with portions in mind
Décor	

Molding cakes

Cake ring	Closed molds

Icing cakes

Two coats	Cake comb

Gelatin-based Fillings

Advance preparation

Assembling a traditional layer cake
Slicing the layers   Consistency/Amount of the filling
Straightening the layers

Glazing a cake
Thin seal coat   Wire rack   Consistency/Temperature of the glaze
Removing air bubbles

Marzipan and other rolled icings
Preparing the surface of the cake   Rolling the marzipan

Self Study Questions

True/False

_____ 1. Cake does not need to be cooled completely before being cut into layers.

_____ 2. Simple syrups are used to moisten the layers of a cake.

_____ 3. Garnishes add visual appeal and act as a flavor indicator.

_____ 4. Dipping a mold in warm water will help to release the cake.

_____ 5. Buttercream is an example of a filling for a traditional layer cake.

Multiple Choice

1. A mousse filling should never be paired with a
      a. chiffon cake
      b. napoleon
      c. pound cake
      d. wedding cake

2. A _____ knife is most suitable for slicing a cake into layers.
      a. chefs knife
      b. paring knife
      c. tourne knife
      d. long, serrated knife

3. A cake ring is also known as a/an
    a. entremet ring
    b. molding ring
    c. roulade
    d. icing ring

4. The sides of a cake are often garnished with
    a. chopped nuts
    b. chocolate shavings
    c. cake crumbs
    d. all of the above

Fill in the blank

1. Fillings that are spread onto the layers of a cake should be less than _____ thick and should not _____ the thickness of the cake layers.

2. A syrup added to a sponge cake adds _____ and _____.

3. A _____ mold, such as a _____, can be used to prepare a bomb or charlotte.

4. Moving a propane torch quickly over the surface of a glazed cake can remove unwanted _____.

Written/Short Answer

1. List the functions of a garnish.

2. Describe the steps taken to glaze a cake.

CHAPTER 17

BREAKFAST PASTRIES

Chapter Overview
For generations, Europeans have reveled in the pastries they enjoy each morning. In France, viennoiseries, or baked products that are sweeter and heavier than bread, are typically eaten at breakfast. Breakfast pastries include everything from flaky croissants to crisp, fruit-filled Danish to moist blueberry muffins.

Chapter Objectives
After reading and studying this chapter, you should be able to:
> - Identify the differences between croissant and Danish doughs.
> - Understand the lamination process.
> - Understand the handling of laminated pastries.
> - Master the technique of shaping coffee cakes.
> - Explain the methods and garnishes used in the preparation of breakfast pastries.

Study Outline

Key Terms and Concepts
Croissant and Danish Doughs

Ingredient ratios	Lamination	Proof

Coffee Cakes

Garnishes	Shaping

Muffins

Creaming Method	Garnishes

Self Study Questions

True/False
_____ 1. Finished croissant and Danish are crisp like puff pastry.

_____ 2. After proofing, shaped croissants and Danish should be nearly double in volume.

_____ 3. Coffee cakes can be made with Danish dough.

Multiple Choice

1. Muffins are typically made using
   a. the creaming method
   b. lamination
   c. proofing
   d. Danish dough

2. Brushing Danish dough with a clear fruit glaze after baking
   a. increases moisture
   b. gives greater flavor
   c. enhances visual appeal
   d. all of the above

3. Vienoisserie are
   a. baked products
   b. sweeter and heavier than bread
   c. generally eaten for breakfast
   d. all of the above

Fill in the Blank

1. Clean cuts on laminated products ensure that they _____.

2. The delicate and flaky texture of croissant and Danish is created by maintaining distinct layers of _____ throughout the process.

Written/Short Answer

1. Describe how croissant and Danish doughs differ.

CHAPTER 18

INDIVIDUAL PASTRIES

Chapter Overview
Individual pastries, created from pastry doughs or batters with fillings, may be constructed as single portions or as a larger item, such as a cake, which is individually garnished and portioned. Individual pastries encompass a wide variety of baked goods, from very refined to rustic. Depending on the type of pastry, it may be appropriate for sale in a retail bakeshop, for service during breakfast or brunch, with coffee or tea, at receptions, or on a dessert menu.

Chapter Objectives
After reading and studying this chapter, the student should be able to:
➤ Prepare a variety of tartlets
➤ Explain the process for poaching fruit
➤ Master the assembly of layered cakes and roulades
➤ Describe the styles and materials available for creating molded pastries
➤ Master the selection of containers for individual pastries
➤ Produce pastries using phyllo dough.
➤ Prepare piped pastries using pâte à choux and baked meringue.
➤ Create pastries using croissant and Danish doughs

Study Outline

Key Terms and Concepts
Tartlets
Scaling down formulas

Poaching Fruits
Fruits suitable for poaching   Poaching liquid

Layered Pastries and Roulades
Slice

Molded Pastries
Flexible molds

Containers
Glass   Natural

Phyllo Dough

Handling of phyllo dough

Piped Pastries
Baked meringue   Pâte à choux

Self Study Questions

True/False

_____ 1. Pre-baked tartlet shells should be left in the ring molds while they are filled in order to support them during assembly and until the filling sets.

_____ 2. Bananas are well-suited to poaching.

_____ 3. Roulades are made from stiff sheets of cake.

_____ 4. Flexible molds made of silicone are used for making molded desserts.

_____ 5. A natural container, such as a hollowed out fruit, is an attractive choice for a pastry container.

Multiple Choice
1. A tartlet may be filled with
    a. fruit
    b. ganache
    c. custard
    d. all of the above

2. When preparing fruits for poaching you should always
    a. wash the fruit
    b. prebake the fruit
    c. wash the fruit, remove the peel and/or seeds
    d. score the skin of the fruit

3. Adding _____ to a mousse will help it to become stable after it is unmolded.
    a. starch
    b. cream
    c. egg whites
    d. gelatin

4. Phyllo dough is made from what basic ingredients?
    a. water, yeast, and flour
    b. flour and water
    c. flour and oil
    d. flour, water, and butter

5. An example of a piped pastry is a
    a. Paris-Brest
    b. bomb
    c. napoleon
    d. petite four

Fill in the blank

1. Tartlets can be baked in a mold or _____.

2. _____ or _____ are puff pastry cases used as pastry containers.

3. A napoleon is an example of a _____.

Written/Short Answer

1. Discuss some unusual or attractive containers for presenting and serving special pastries and other desserts.

CHAPTER 19

SAVORY BAKING

Chapter Overview
Savory baking enables the pastry chef to deepen the professional repertoire. Execution of these products will broaden the understanding of how savory baked goods can provide an opportunity for lighter dining, creative amuse plates, and nourishing accompaniment to an informal gathering, cocktail reception, or large-scale catering event.

Chapter Objectives
After reading and studying this chapter, you should be able to:
- ➢ Explain the importance of savory for a pastry chef or baker.
- ➢ Discuss flavor profiles and food trends.
- ➢ Understand and execute basic knife cuts for fresh herbs and vegetables.
- ➢ Know the differences between the cooking methods and know what type of product is suitable for each.
- ➢ Execute all of the different cooking methods.

Study Outline

Key Terms and Concepts
The Importance of Savory for a Pastry Chef or Baker
Flavor profiles   Food trends

Cutting Vegetables and Fresh Herbs
Chop	Mince	Chiffonade	Julienne
Batonnet	Brunoise	Dice	

Cooking Methods
Sauté	Sauté pan	Sweat	Steam	Grill
Broil	Roast	Barding	Larding	Pan frying
Deep frying				

Self Study Questions

True/False

_____ 1. The julienne cut is used for leafy vegetables and herbs.

_____ 2. Sautéing is a technique that cooks food rapidly in a little fat over relatively high heat.

_____ 3. A sauté pan has tall, straight sides.

_____ 4. When grilling or broiling use a smaller cut of meat than if you were roasting or baking.

_____ 5. Roasting food results in a crusty exterior and tender interior.

_____ 6. Wild game such as venison, boar, and game birds are often barded or larded.

_____ 7. Food that will be deep fried is usually coated in a batter.

Multiple Choice

1. The desired outcome of sweating is
    a. softening with no color
    b. some browning on the edges
    c. deep caramelization
    d. none of the above

2. Tougher cuts of meat are usually used in
    a. sautéing
    b. pan frying
    c. steaming
    d. none of the above

3. The knife cut with the dimensions 1/8 by 1/8 by 1/8 is
    a. brunoise
    b. julienne
    c. fine julienne
    d. batonnet

4. Drippings left in the pan used to make sauces are called
    a. mirepoix
    b. fond
    c. paysanne
    d. court bouillon

Fill in the Blank

1. In broiling the heat source comes from _____ the food.

2. Common ingredients in batters for frying include _____, _____ and _____.

91

Written/Short Answer

1. Explain the sequence in dicing any type of vegetable.

2. Explain how to sauté as well as what type of meat is best suited for it.

3. Describe the difference between sautéing and searing.

4. What does it mean to "sweat" vegetables?

Essay

1. Indicate the difference between pan frying and deep frying.

CHAPTER 20

PLATED DESSERTS

Chapter Overview
When designing a plated dessert, the pastry chef must consider the composition, exploring the possibilities of contrasting and complementing flavors and textures as well as color and style. Equally important to consider are the customer base, specific event or menu needs, and the environment for preparation and service.

Chapter Objectives
After reading and studying this chapter, you should be able to:
➤ Discuss trends in plated desserts.
➤ Explain the pastry contrast table.
➤ Master dessert station mise en place.
➤ Identify factors that contribute to the creation of a restaurant dessert menu.
➤ Select plated desserts suitable for banquets.
➤ Understand the use of frozen components in a plated dessert.

Study Outline

Key Terms and Concepts
Trends in Plated Desserts

Architectural style	Rustic-style

The Contrast Table

Flavor	Taste	Texture	Temperature
Eye Appeal			

Restaurant Desserts

Kitchen Setup	Seasonality

Dessert Station Mise en Place

Size and configuration	Location and physical access	Efficient workflow

Plating Frozen Desserts

Edible Containers	Freezer Space

Plated Desserts at Banquets

Plating	Equipment	Storage
Timing of service	Labor	

Self Study Questions

True/False

_____ 1. When designing a dessert menu, it is essential to consider current trends to keep your menu fresh and interesting.

_____ 2. The pastry contrast table is a visual guide to understanding the basic characteristics that can be used by the pastry chef in the creation of plated desserts.

_____ 3. All items on a restaurant's dessert menu should change seasonally.

_____ 4. It is not a good idea to have a container with double-strength sanitizing solution available on a dessert station.

Multiple Choice

1. Current trends in desserts include
   - a. low-fat options
   - b. architectural style
   - c. rustic-style
   - d. both b and c

2. Seasonality plays an important role in the creation of plated desserts because
   - a. it ensures best possible flavor
   - b. it keeps costs and prices down
   - c. the freshest items will appeal more to customers
   - d. all of the above

3. When setting up a work station, it is important to consider
   - a. the size and configuration of the area
   - b. the colors and textures of the plated dessert
   - c. the number of waiters
   - d. often-used items be stored out of reach.

Fill in the Blank

1. The object of a textural component is to have a balance of _____.

2. The appeal of home-style desserts lies in their simplicity of _____, _____, and _____.

3. The _____ makes waiters aware of the food, which causes items to sell better.

Written/Short Answer

1. List 3 important factors in setting up a dessert station.

CHAPTER 21

CHOCOLATES AND CONFECTIONS

Chapter Overview
This chapter introduces principles and techniques involved with working with chocolate and sugar. These techniques are used to make ganaches, gianduja, caramels, candied fruit, fondant, marzipan, and gelées, as well as aerated, molded, and deposited candies, chocolates and other confections.

Chapter Objectives
After reading and studying this chapter, you should be able to:
- ➤ Explain the basic principles cream and egg ganache preparation
- ➤ Prepare flavored ganache for truffles
- ➤ Describe proper preparation techniques for forming truffles and other ganache confections.
- ➤ Explain the proper procedure for melting chocolate.
- ➤ Prepare tempered chocolate
- ➤ Describe the steps for preparing molded chocolates
- ➤ Describe the method for making dragées
- ➤ Prepare rochers and knackerli
- ➤ Explain the procedure for cooking sugar to different stages
- ➤ Prepare soft caramels and brittle

Study Outline

Key Terms and Concepts
Melting Chocolate

Finely chopped	hot water bath	seize
microwave		

Working with Couverature
Temperature

Tempering Chocolate

Cooling	agitation	fat crystals
Seed method	block method	tabling method

Cream Ganache

Cocoa solids	recrystalization	infusion

Butter Ganache
Tempered chocolate

Egg Ganache

Forming Truffles and other ganache confections

Agitation	scoop	piping
Frame	guitar	

Dipping Confections

Dipping fork	foot	décor
Dusting	spiking	transfer sheets
Pre-made shells		

Molding chocolates

Couverture	semisolid consistency

Rochers

Knackerli

Gianduja

Dragées

Cooking Sugar to Different Stages

Wet method	acid	Thread
Soft ball	firm ball	hard ball
Soft crack	hard crack	caramel

Soft Caramel

Peanut Brittle

Hard Candies

Self Study Questions

True/False

_____ 1. Cream ganache may be used as a glaze for cakes and pastries.

_____ 2. Corn syrup should never be used in cream ganache.

_____ 3. Tempered chocolate should be malleable when set.

_____ 4. Truffles should have a thick coating of tempered chocolate.

_____ 5. Sugar reaches the thread stage between 215 and 230 degrees Fahrenheit.

Multiple Choice

1. The ratio of dark chocolate to heavy cream for making ganache is
    a. 2:1
    b. 1:2
    c. 1:8
    d. 8:1

2. Ganache may be portioned by
    a. piping
    b. scooping
    c. spooning
    d. a and b
    e. a and c

3. Couverture has a minimum of _____ percent cocoa butter.
    a. 32%
    b. 44%
    c. 53%
    d. 62%

4. Chocolate truffles should have _____ coatings of tempered chocolate.
    a. 6
    b. 2
    c. 4
    d. 3

5. An example of a sweetener used for making butter ganache is
    a. jam
    b. confectioners' sugar
    c. granulated sugar
    d. light brown sugar

6. Soft caramels may be flavored with
    a. coffee beans
    b. pastes
    c. spices
    d. both a and c
    d. all of the above

Fill in the Blank
1. Couverture is chocolate that contains a minimum of _____ percent _____.

2. After it has been portioned, ganache must be allowed to set _____ until firm.

3. _____ and _____ may be added to ganache to help prevent recrystallization.

4. Tempering chocolate is achieved through _____ and _____.

5. The sweetener used for butter ganache must be _____.

6. To cook sugar to a specific stage is must be cooked by the _____ method.

Short Answer / Essay

1. Describe the process for infusing flavors into a cream ganache.

2. List three methods for tempering chocolate.

3. List the advantages of using pre-made truffle shells

CHAPTER 22

DÉCOR

Chapter Overview
Décor is the finishing touch given to any pastry or cake. The pastry chef employs a variety of techniques and materials to craft a look that not only displays creativity and skill but also sets his or her pastries, cakes, and other desserts apart.

Chapter Objectives
After reading and studying this chapter, you should be able to:
- ➢ Master the techniques for piping borders and flowers
- ➢ Prepare a parchment piping bag
- ➢ Master the techniques for piping tempered chocolate
- ➢ Make tempered chocolate cutouts and stencils
- ➢ Produce décor using royal icing
- ➢ Make marzipan, marzipan flowers, and marzipan plaques
- ➢ Master the techniques for spun, pulled, and blown sugar
- ➢ Prepare garnishes using sugar pastes

Study Outline

Key Terms and Concepts
Tools for Décor
Coupler

Piping buttercream borders and flowers

Tempered Chocolate Décor
Spread-and-cut method

Working with Royal Icing
String work   Flood work and run-outs

Marzipan
Mélangeur

Working with Sugar Pastes
Pastillage   Gum paste

Self Study Questions

True/False

_____1. Décor is the finishing touch given to any pastry or cake.

_____2. A coupler is a tool used to make tempered chocolate stencils and cutouts.

Multiple Choice
1. The main ingredient used to make marzipan is
   - a. almond paste
   - b. butter cream
   - c. royal icing
   - d. ground hazelnuts

2. Stencils and cutouts may be made of
   - a. white chocolate
   - b. milk chocolate
   - c. dark chocolate
   - d. all of the above

Fill in the Blank
1. Parchment paper used to make piping cones should be cut into _____ inch rectangles, or _____ inch rectangles for smaller cones.
2. _____ is typically piped in parchment or plastic sheets, allowed to dry, and stored in airtight containers for later use.

Written/Short Answer
1. Describe how to make a parchment piping cone.

CHAPTER 23

WEDDING AND SPECIALTY CAKES

Chapter Overview
Wedding and specialty cakes are a culmination of the talent, skills, and knowledge of the pastry chef or baker. To make a beautiful and flavorful cake, the pastry chef or baker must hone his or her skills in almost all aspects of the baking and pastry arts. Creation and development of cakes such as the ones in this chapter are limited only by the creativity of the individual.

Chapter Objectives
After reading and studying this chapter, you should be able to:
> Define the traditional and the modern wedding cake.
> Prepare specialty cakes.
> Master the techniques for building a properly supported cake.
> Describe the production schedule for wedding and specialty cakes.
> Explain the process for transporting the cake to job sites.
> Determine the cost for wedding cakes.

Study Outline

Key Terms and Concepts
Traditional Wedding Cakes

British-style	Australian-style	South African-style

The Modern Wedding Cake

Specialty Cakes

Building a Properly Supported Cake

Scheduling the Production of a Wedding or Specialty Cake

Transporting the Cake
Nonskid carpet pad

Costing Wedding Cakes

Labor cost	Market segment/location	Food cost
Unique features		

Self Study Questions

Written/Short Answer

1. Make a schedule for the production of a wedding or specialty cake.

2. What is the difference between a wedding cake and a specialty cake?